"The Girl at the Mirror"
by Norman Rockwell

Windows of the Soul

Experiencing God in New Ways

KEN GIRE

ZondervanPublishingHouse
Grand Rapids, Michigan

A Division of HarperCollins*Publishers*

Windows of the Soul
Copyright © 1996 by Ken Gire, Jr.

Requests for information should be addressed to:

⚏ ZondervanPublishingHouse
Grand Rapids, Michigan 49530

Library of Congress Cataloging-in-Publication Data

Gire, Ken.
  Windows of the soul : experiencing God in new ways / Ken Gire.
      p.   cm.
  ISBN: 0-310-20397-X (hardcover)
  1.Soul. 2. Experience (Religion) 3. Spiritual life—Christianity. I. Title.
BT741.2.G57   1996
248.2-dc 20   96-46899
                                                                                 CIP

International Trade Paper Edition 0-310-20972-2

This edition printed on acid-free paper and meets the American National
Standards Institute Z39.48 standard.

Edited by Bob Hudson
Interior design by Sue Vandenberg-Koppenol

Printed in the United States of America

---

96 97 98 99 00 01 02 /❖/ 10 9 8 7 6 5 4 3 2 1

Dedicated to Lee Hough
My wish for every reader
is a friend as good as he

Special thanks to Ann Spangler
Senior Acquisitions Editor at Zondervan
for suggesting this project,
thinking enough of me to believe
I might have something to say
on a topic as important as this

A *Prayer* Before Writing

To speak of the soul with certainty seems a child's boast.
Who can know for certain what is there in our innermost being?
Who can know for certain what isn't?
And if we can't plumb the depths of our own being,
  how can we begin to fathom You, O God?
To write of such things is like a child who runs through the surf,
  kicking up a lot of spray
    yet knowing so little of the sea.
With a child's vocabulary I approach a subject too deep for words.
Is it a child's attempt to sound very grown up?
  Talkative and very sure of himself.
Or is it a child's step toward growing up?
  Tentative and unsure.
I don't know.
Maybe something of both.
Whatever the reason, Lord, watch over that child
  and over the words he has gathered
    like so many broken shells along the shore.
Please smooth the edges of those that are sharp
  and let them find hands that will treasure them
    even in their brokenness.

Contents

Introduction

It hardly seems possible to talk about the soul without in some way talking about God. Something like a tour guide taking you through St. Peter's Cathedral, pointing out the intricate design of the architecture, the polished craftsmanship of the woodwork, and the painstaking artistry of the stained glass, all the while never mentioning why the cathedral was built in the first place.

It is, I suppose, possible to speak of the soul without speaking of God, just as it is possible to tour a cathedral without stopping to worship. Most of us, though, have taken that tour. And for most of us, it's not enough.

The pursuit of self is what most of us have been doing for much of our lives, even our spiritual lives. But the self is a cul-de-sac, and eventually we end up where we started. Footsore and just as frustrated, just as unfulfilled. Feeling we're a failure, or worse, a fraud.

The pursuit of soul, if soul is all we're pursuing, is not much different. It's a longer walk down a nicer street, but the street is still a cul-de-sac, and in the end, regardless how invigorating the walk, it doesn't lead beyond the neighborhood of who we are.

Most of us, though, have grown a little tired of the neighborhood and all the back-and-forth trips we've taken there. We long for something more than a routine walk around the religious block.

We long for the companionship of God.

We long for the assurance that we are not taking this journey alone. That He is walking with us and talking with us and intimately involved in our lives.

We have all had moments when we've experienced something of that intimacy. Moments we can't quite explain, yet can't explain away. Moments when God has touched our lives like a soft hand of morning sun reaching through our bedroom window, brushing over our eyes, and waking us to something eternal.

At some of these windows, what we see offers simply a moment of insight, making us slower to judge and quicker to show understanding. At a

11

few of them, though, what we see offers a word spoken to the very depths of who we are. It may be a word to rouse us from sleep and ready us for our life's journey. It may be a word to warn us of a precipice or guide us to a place of rest. It may be a word telling us who we are and why we are here and what is required of us at this particular juncture of our journey.

Or, in a startling sun-drenched moment of grace, it may be a word telling us something we have longed all of our lives to hear—a word from God—a word so precious it would be worth the most arduous of climbs to hear the least audible of its echoes.

Windows of the soul is where we hear those words.

And where the journey begins.

Part One

Windows of the Soul

A glass window stands before us. We raise our eyes and see the glass; we note its quality, and observe its defects; we speculate on its composition. Or we look straight through it on the great prospect of land and sea and sky beyond.

BENJAMIN B. WARFIELD
"Some Thoughts on Predestination"

God stretched out the heavens, stippling the night with impressionistic stars. He set the sun to the rhythm of the day, the moon to the rhythm of the month, the seasons to the rhythm of the year. He blew wind through reedy marshes and beat drums of distant thunder. He formed a likeness of Himself from a lump of clay and into it breathed life. He crafted a counterpart to complete the likeness, joining the two halves and placing them center stage in His creation where there was a temptation and a fall, a great loss and a great hiding. God searched for the hiding couple, reaching to pick them up, dust them off, draw them near. Though they hardly knew it at the time. After them, He searched for their children and for their children's children. And afterward wrote stories of His search.

In doing all this, God gave us art, music, sculpture, drama, and literature. He gave them as footpaths to lead us out of our hiding places and as signposts to lead us along in our search for what was lost.

Shaped from something of earth and something of heaven, we were torn between two worlds. A part of us wanted to hide. A part of us wanted to search. With half-remembered words still legible in our hearts and faintly sketched images still visible in our souls, some of us stepped out of hiding and started our search.

Though we hardly knew where to look.

We painted to see if what was lost was in the picture. We composed to hear if what was lost was in the music. We sculpted to find if what was lost was in the stone. We wrote to discover if what was lost was in the story.

Through art and music and stories we searched for what was missing from our lives.

Though at times we hardly knew it.

Though at times we could hardly keep from knowing it.

The German poet Rilke tells of one of those times in a fable where the sculpting hands of Michelangelo "tore at the stone as at a grave, in which a faint dying voice is flickering. 'Michelangelo,' cried God in dread, 'who is in the stone?' Michelangelo listened; his hands were trembling. Then he answered in a muffled voice: 'Thou, my God, who else? But I cannot reach Thee.'"

We reach for God in many ways. Through our sculptures and our scriptures. Through our pictures and our prayers. Through our writing and our worship. And through them He reaches for us.

His search begins with something said. Ours begins with something heard. His begins with something shown. Ours, with something seen. Our search for God and His search for us meet at windows in our everyday experience.

These are the windows of the soul.

In a sense, it is something like spiritual disciplines for the spiritually undisciplined. In another sense, it is the most rigorous of disciplines—the discipline of awareness. For we must always be looking and listening if we are to see the windows and hear what is being spoken to us through them.

But we must learn to look with more than just our eyes and listen with more than just our ears, for the sounds are sometimes faint and the sights sometimes far away. We must be aware, at all times and in all places, because windows are everywhere, and at any time we may find one.

Or one may find us.

Though we will hardly know it . . . unless we are searching for Him who for so long has been searching for us.

When we look long enough at a scene from a movie, a page from a book, a person from across the room, and when we look deeply enough, those moments framed in our minds grow transparent. Everywhere we look, there are pictures that are not really pictures but windows. If only we have eyes to see beyond the paint. If we look closely, we can see something beyond the two dimensions within the frame, something beyond the ordinary colors brushed across the canvas of our everyday lives.

What do we see in those windows? What do we see of who we are, or once were, or one day might become? What do we see of our neighbor living down the street or our neighbor living *on* the street? What do we see about God?

Windows of the soul is a way of seeing that begins with respect. The way we show respect is to give it a second look, a look not of the eyes but of the heart. But so often we don't give something a second look because we don't think there is anything there to see.

To respect something is to understand that there is something there to see, that it is not all surface, that something lies beneath the surface, something that has the power to change the way we think or feel, something that may prove so profound a revelation as to change not only how we look at our lives but how we live them.

Jesus lived His life that way, seeing beyond the pictures of the widow at Nain and the woman at the well, of the tax collector in the tree and the thief on the cross, of the rich man and Lazarus.

He was constantly looking beyond the two dimensions of the full-sized portraits framed before him. Beyond the widow's tears for her dead son, Jesus saw how much she needed that son to fill the hole left by her deceased husband. Beyond the Samaritan woman's veil, He saw the five marriages that had failed, and beyond that, the emptiness in her life that grew bigger with each divorce. Beyond the power and wealth of Zacchaeus, He saw a small man with a big hole in his heart that all the power and wealth in the world couldn't fill. Beyond the sores of Lazarus, He saw a soul of eternal worth. Beyond the clothes of the rich man, He saw a soul in rags.

Seeing windows of the soul was the way Jesus lived His life and the way He taught His disciples to live theirs. One of those lessons came at the Temple treasury. The treasury was located in the Court of the Women, a place of worship set aside for them because they were restricted from worshiping with the men. Twelve trumpet-shaped receptacles were located there so both groups could have equal access.

When large donations of coins clinked into those receptacles, it turned heads, and the heads took note. Treasury officials kept good mental records of the top donors, making sure they were shown the proper respect, greeted deferentially in the streets, seated preferentially in the synagogues. Lesser donors went unnoticed.

But not today. Not by Jesus anyway. He frames the following picture of what He sees.

A widow in worn-out clothes shuffles by and gives as her offering a couple of copper coins. The tiny coins, together worth only a fraction of a cent, drop into the coffers without sound or spectacle. And she shuffles away.

A few drab brush strokes; that's all there is to the picture. But that's enough for Jesus. He looks beneath its freshly painted surface and calls His disciples to make sure they see this window of the soul.

"I tell you the truth, this poor widow has put more into the treasury than all the others. They all gave out of their wealth; but she, out of her poverty, put in everything—all she had to live on."

The widow had nothing to live on and no one to look after her. Her concern wasn't a mortgage payment; it was her next meal. That's why the offering was so extraordinary. The fraction of a cent represented the focus of her life. It represented not only her faithfulness in helping to provide for God's work but also her faith in God to provide for her. It was a beautiful picture, but a picture only Jesus and His disciples saw. The eyes of everyone else were attracted to more public displays.

Someone once said that the spiritual significance of something is in inverse proportion to the publicity surrounding it. A publicized event, like a parade, is more spectacular than it is significant. And that is true even if the parade is a religious one.

"When you give to the needy," Jesus said, "do not announce it with trumpets as the hypocrites do in the synagogues and on the streets, to be honored by men. I tell you the truth, they have received their reward in full. But when you give to the needy, do not let your left hand know what your right hand is doing, so that your giving may be in secret. Then your Father, who sees what is done in secret, will reward you."

If such things as art galleries exist in heaven, certainly the picture of the widow's offering is hanging there in a prominent place, for it was one of those secret acts of devotion that Christ referred to, something sacred that the Father saw and treasured.

"To sense the sacred," said Abraham Heschel, "is to sense what is dear to God." The Temple, which for so long had been a sacred place, had become a streetside gallery of religious display. Lost behind the clutter of ornately framed gestures was a pencil sketch of a poor widow's soul. Not until Jesus pulled it out and put a frame around it did the disciples even realize it was there. Once they did, though, they sensed it was a sacred picture, revealing to them a window and showing them what was dear to God.

How does a person learn to see like that, to look beyond the rags of a widow to the riches of her heart, to see in the everyday moments of life something of eternal worth?

We learn from the artists, from those who work in paint or words or musical notes, from those who have eyes that see and ears that hear and hearts that feel deeply and passionately about all that is sacred and dear to God.

To learn to see the way an artist sees takes time. A long time, in my case. There is a story behind the picture in the front of this book that tells something of the process. It is a Norman Rockwell, titled *Girl at the Mirror*. It first appeared on the cover of the *Saturday Evening Post* magazine on March 6, 1954.

I was four.

If my mother had a copy lying around the house, I never saw it, or if I did, I never gave it a second look. And if by chance I gave it a second look, I never gave it a second thought. What I looked at in those days was Saturday morning cartoons not the *Saturday Evening Post*. What I thought about was Roy Rogers not Norman Rockwell. *Gunsmoke* not *Girl at the Mirror*.

A lot has changed in forty years.

I have forgotten the cartoons and the cowboys and the gunfights. But not the *Girl at the Mirror*.

I first saw a print of the picture years ago. I looked at it as I looked at most things back then, seeing what use I could make of it. I could put it over the sofa my wife's grandmother had given us. The greens would match the fabric, almost, and blend with the sculptured avocado carpet. Give the apartment a homier look.

But that was just a thought, and I never gave it a second one.

Did you, when you first saw it in the front of the book? If you skipped over it, as I once did, go back and look again. Let's look at it together, and together we'll try to look beyond the paint.

The painting seems to be saying something, revealing something. But what?

I look. I listen. I ask questions.

The room in the picture is mostly dark. Why? The mirror is propped up by a chair. Why? Is this the girl's room, her parents' room, a bathroom? An attic maybe? The lighting probably wouldn't be very good in an attic. And if there were a mirror there, it probably wouldn't be hanging on a wall but leaning against something, a box or a chair. Yes, I think it is an attic.

But why is the girl looking at a mirror in the attic and not at a mirror, say, in the bathroom or the bedroom or the hall? Is she hiding? If so, from whom? Is she afraid? If so, of what?

I look closer. Lipstick on the floor, opened. Is it hers? Her mother's? A brush and a comb and, what is that behind them—a hand-held mirror?

She has a magazine on her lap. Opened to a picture of a woman. Dark hair. Like hers. Who is it? A mother, a teacher? Actress, I think. Yes. Maureen? No. Rosalind Russell? No, Jane . . . Jane Russell. That's it. Film star.

The girl is barefoot and wearing a slip. Did she go to the attic to play dress-up and then see the magazine? Or did she bring the magazine with her? A doll lies off to the side, in a heap. Was it there already, or did she bring it with her? Did she toss it to the floor, consciously, or did it slip from her hand, unconsciously, as she propped up the mirror?

She sits close to that mirror. What does she see? What does she think about what she sees? Why are her arms drawn in? And her hands. Why are they held where they are and the way they are? Why isn't she posing? Or smiling? What all is going on behind those dark eyes in the mirror?

There is something about this girl, this girl whose arms are held close and whose hands are curled inward like the petals of a flower. She is somewhere between bud and blossom. Somewhere between her last doll and her first date. Somewhere between dressing up and growing up.

And there is something sad about that.

Something of that sadness is in her face, in her eyes. Can you see it? There is also something of shyness. Maybe that's why she's in the attic. And there are quiet, unspoken fears coming from those dark eyes that seem to make the attic even darker. Can you sense it?

What is she afraid of? And why?

The girl is at a threshold in her life, standing on very tentative legs, now sitting. She knows it is a threshold she will have to cross, but she's hesitant, unsure. Her body is tugging at her, pulling her through the door, but something inside is pulling her back.

She's wondering, I think, about a lot of things. Wondering what lies ahead. Wondering what, besides the doll, she will have to leave behind. Wondering if she'll make it as a grown-up, if she'll be accepted into that world. Wondering how she'll turn out, what she'll look like. Will her face be a magazine face, someday? Or will it forever be the face in the mirror?

She wonders.

What do you feel when you see her sitting there in front of that mirror, with her doll forgotten on the floor? Tenderness? Compassion? Understanding? And where do those feelings lead? Don't you want to sit down beside her, put your arm around her, tell her a story of when you were her age and the thoughts you had then, the fears you had then?

There is something about this girl, something about her that is about all of us. For all of us go through life from one threshold to another. And at those thresholds, most of us stand on very tentative legs, wanting to take a step, but we're hesitant, unsure. We wonder what lies ahead? And what has to be left behind in getting there?

In moving to a new house, we have to say good-bye to the old neighborhood, old friends, old memories. In going off to college, we have to leave our home and family behind. In getting married, we have to shed something of our independence. In starting a career, we have to leave behind college and those special times, those special friends, that cloistered sense of security. In starting a family, we have to close the chapter on the relatively uncomplicated, uninterrupted life we had as a childless couple. In getting a promotion, we have to leave behind a job we love, maybe, or a city we love, or a state. In our children going off to college or to careers or to start families of their own, something is left behind when they leave, something precious, something we and they can come back to only in stories and scrapbooks. In retiring, we bid a final farewell to our livelihood, and though our friends at work remain our friends, a dimension of those friendships is also left behind.

We go from threshold to threshold with something pulling us forward and something pulling us back. We sit in front of a mirror, tentative, hesitant, unsure.

How does God feel about us when He sees us at one of those thresholds, sitting in front of one of those mirrors? Does He feel less tenderness than we felt for the girl at the mirror? What is He wanting to tell us at those very insecure, very fearful times? "Grow up. Get a grip. Get up and get on with your life." Is that what He's wanting to say?

Or is He wanting to sit beside us, put an arm around our waist, and tell us a story of the thresholds His own son had to step across, at Bethlehem, at the Jordan River, and at Gethsemane? Times when His son also felt something pulling Him forward and something pulling Him back. Times when He also was tentative, unsure, and yes, even afraid.

There have been many thresholds in my own life, and doubtless there will be many more. Some have been easier to cross than others, and on some I just sat there, feeling very alone and very afraid. Looking back, though, I don't think I was alone. I think God was sitting beside me. And I think, or hope anyway, that He felt something for me that was more tender, more compassionate, and more understanding than what I felt for that girl in the mirror.

That is why the picture is for me a window of the soul.

And that is why I can't forget it.

A Prayer for Awareness

Thank You, O God,

For seeing beyond the surface of my life
  to the child sitting at the mirror.
Thank You for sitting down beside me,
    putting Your arm around me,
        and speaking to me with such tenderness,
          such compassion, and such understanding.
Help me to be aware of the pictures in my life
    that are everywhere around me and at all times
        showing me something I need to see,
        telling me something I need to hear,
        offering me something I need to receive.
Help me look beyond the surface of those pictures to see windows.
Give me eyes to see, ears to hear, and a heart to receive
    what You are offering me through those windows,
        that I might sense what is dear to You
            so that it might become what is dear to me . . .

Pausing at the Window

The problem is not entirely in finding the room of one's own, the time alone, difficult and necessary as that is. The problem is more how to still the soul in the midst of its activities.

ANNE MORROW LINDBERGH
Gift from the Sea

Windows of the soul offer glimpses, however fleeting, and echoes, however faint, of some of the things that are dear to God.

I caught one of those glimpses on a Sunday afternoon obscured with activity. It should have been a day to push back the papers that cluttered the desk of my soul, but the papers were urgent and I was anxious. I was behind on a writing project with a fast-approaching deadline, so I had set aside Sunday afternoon to spend catching up.

Early that afternoon, though, my daughter asked if I would take her to see a friend who was playing in a roller hockey game. The friend was a boy whom I'll call Joey. He had cerebral palsy, my daughter said, and he had asked her at school Friday if she would come and watch him play. She told him she would, if she could get a ride.

As it turned out, I was the only ride available.

I said yes, knowing if I didn't, that something precious would be lost, and though I didn't know what that was, I knew it was greater than whatever could be gained by saying no.

When we arrived at the roller rink, I went in with her, thinking I could find a quiet nook and get some work done. But inside, all kinds of noises echoed off the bare walls and slatted wood floor. Video arcades lined one of the walls, luring young boys with loose change. A concession stand lined another, luring the rest of us. Families of the players milled around, talking, several of them leaning against the perimeter railing.

I was looking for an out-of-the-way place to write when my daughter pointed out Joey. He was playing goalie, hidden behind shin guards, face mask, and a chest guard. He had been positioned where he didn't have to move much, so I hardly noticed he was handicapped. All I noticed was that he stood a foot taller and years older than the other players.

Gathered at the railing behind Joey were four boys from my daughter's school. She joined them while I nested in a vacant table, taking out my pen and notebook, busying myself with all the catching up I had scheduled for that afternoon. But the sight of those five high school kids and the sound of their cheering distracted me. I stopped and paused and wondered if there was something I should be paying attention to, something that might prove to be a window of the soul.

I turned to a fresh page.

I watched. I listened. And I framed the moment with words.

"Way to go, Joey," one of the boys calls out.

The other team scores against him.

"It's all right, Joey."

Joey blocks a shot.

The five high school kids cheer. "Way to go, Joey."

The game goes back and forth from the far goal to the near one. Joey shows dissatisfaction with the way he's playing.

"Don't worry, Joey."

The four boys sit clumped on a round table. My daughter is off to the side. Joey makes another save, and all of them cheer. My daughter finally gets tired of standing and sits on the table with the boys.

"Way to hustle. Great defense. Yeah."

"Good job, Joey."

One by one they get up and lean on the railing, closer to the action. Joey pounds the floor with his hockey stick.

"Joey, you're doing great."

In a letter dated October 10, 1907, the poet Rilke talks about his first exposure to the artwork of Cezanne, how he spent hours in front of his pictures, looking, listening, trying to understand them: "I remember the puzzlement and insecurity of one's first confrontation with his work, along with his name, which is just as new. And then for a long time nothing, and suddenly one has the right eyes."

I sat in front of the picture, looking, listening, trying to understand it. For a long time nothing.

Then a memory of the widow at the temple made a silhouette of my thoughts. She was a person no one noticed until Jesus framed her with His words. I thought of the picture of that poor widow. And of the passage where Jesus talks about giving to the poor. Then of Joey.

And suddenly I have the right eyes.

Suddenly I realized that there are many ways a person can be impoverished, and sometimes the least of those ways is materially. That was the case with Joey.

His poverty was not material; it was relational. He didn't need money or what money could buy. He needed something it couldn't buy—friends. He needed, as we all need, friends who will talk to him in the hall and sit with him at lunch and have him over to spend the night. He needed, as we all need, friends who will show up at a crosstown roller rink, lean against the railing, and cheer him on.

Some people are rich in friends like that.

Joey isn't.

Joey is an impoverished kid groping for his soul's daily bread in the halls of his high school. With sometimes lame and socially awkward overtures, he accosts his classmates, holding out his hand for a crust of what they have in such abundance. He begs them to look beyond the disease and all it has robbed him of. He begs them to look beyond the slur of his words and the shuffle of his feet. He begs them to see Joey.

Of course, he can't put it into words like that or into any words close to that. His inarticulate emotions can express themselves only in frustration, bouts of depression, and outbursts of anger. It's the way of the artist, calling to those walking away from his art, begging them to come back and look beyond the paint to see the passion of his soul enflamed on the canvas.

With the language of emotion, a complex and sometimes indecipherable language, Joey is begging us to look beyond the jarring and disjointed Picasso that his life appears to be on the surface, pleading with us to see within him the beautiful and breathtaking Michelangelo, which is no less than the very image of God.

"If we are to love our neighbors," says Frederick Buechner, "before doing anything else we must *see* our neighbors. With our imagination as well as with our eyes, that is to say like artists, we must see not just their faces but the life behind and within their faces."

That day I saw something behind the face of the hockey mask and behind the face of cerebral palsy.

I saw Joey.

Besides Joey, I wondered what else there was to see in that roller rink on that Sunday afternoon. I looked beyond him to the five kids still at the railing. They could have been at the video arcade. They could have been at the concession stand. They could have been at the table, talking among themselves, joking among themselves, preoccupied with themselves. And who could blame them if they were? We would be there ourselves, doing the same things ourselves, wouldn't we?

But they weren't there; they were at the railing. They weren't preoccupied with themselves; they were preoccupied with Joey. Watching him. Encouraging him. Cheering him on.

And as they did, something changed hands. What was it? I squinted. A gift of some sort. A gift Joey desperately needed. Neither the hands of the giver nor the hands of the receiver were aware of the exchange. But the Father who sees in secret, He saw it, He took note of it, He treasured it.

And so did I.

Was that all there was to see in that picture? Or was there more?

I looked again. For a long time nothing. And suddenly again I have the right eyes.

Beyond Joey and beyond the gift that had been given him, I saw a girl who had given up her Sunday afternoon to help give that gift. She had asked to be there. She could have asked to be somewhere else, the mall, the movies, anywhere. But she asked to be there. She told a boy with cerebral palsy she would watch him play if she could find a ride. She found a ride. And she kept a promise to someone for whom promises were not so much broken as they were simply forgotten.

The picture was a window to my daughter's soul, revealing to me something of the secret of who she is, a secret I will need to know if I am to understand her and nurture her and draw out in her all that is dear to God.

That Sunday afternoon in that roller rink I saw something sacred, something dear to God. And in a sudden, somewhat sobering moment, I realized I was the only person on earth who had seen it.

Something about that made me feel special, excited to be alive at just that place and at just that time to see then and there what no one else had seen.

And yet something about being the only one also made me feel sad.

The moment did something to me that I can't quite put my finger on, let alone find words for. Maybe there are no words for such moments in a person's life. Maybe some moments are too sacred for words. What I experienced that day was profoundly moving, and one of the places it moved me was to wonder: How many windows have I missed because I was too busy to look? And how much wisdom have I overlooked because I was too behind in my schedule to even see what was being offered?

The problem is not entirely in finding a quiet nook in this roller rink world of ours. The problem is quieting the soul in the midst of the noise.

But quieting the soul of a writer, who once fed a family of six from odd jobs and sometimes no jobs at all, is no small task. In those days I spent most of my time waiting for better times. I waited for the day the book would get written, and for the day it would get sent off. I waited for the day the publisher would reply, which was most of the time a form letter and all of the time a letter of rejection. I waited for the day when something I wrote would get published. When that day finally came, I continued to wait, partly because by now I was really good at it, and partly at least because I was at a time in my life when I needed to feel I was good at something, even at such a small thing as waiting.

So I waited for the first copy to come from the printer, and when I got it, I waited for the first copies to arrive at the bookstores. After that I waited for the first royalty check to come, to see if I had a career or just lunch money for the next week.

I lived a book at a time, a check at a time, and charted the course for my future, for all six of our futures, from a sextant fixed on just such dim starlight as that.

Someday I would write. Someday I would get something published. Someday I would be a full-time writer, making a living at what I loved. But while I was living for all those somedays, I was missing all my todays. I was so busy getting where I wanted to be I forgot where I was and what was being offered me there by the generous hand of God.

Seeing windows in my day-to-day life changed all that, quieting the noise in my soul as I began to realize not only what was being offered, but by whom. And I began to receive what was offered, not someday but today.

Today, though, has its own whirl of responsibilities, and if we get caught up in the spin, the windows of the soul will blur by us. To keep that from happening, Anne Morrow Lindbergh suggests we strive "to be the still axis within the revolving wheel of relationships, obligations, and activities."

The still axis.

It is able to maintain its center no matter how fast the wheel is turning. It is, in fact, what keeps the wheel turning. Without the axis being still, the wheel would wobble off or else bind up and bring everything lurching to a stop. Stillness is what gives stability. And it is what keeps the wheels from falling off our lives.

The problem is not indigenous to our times, however fast-paced and frenetic those times may seem. The problem is as old as humanity and as ingrained as human nature. Paging back two thousand years and peering through the window of another culture, we see the same problem in the home of two sisters. One is a still axis; the other is caught in a revolving wheel.

As Jesus and his disciples were on their way, He came to a village where a woman named Martha opened her home to Him. She had a sister called Mary, who sat at the Lord's feet, listening to what He said. But Martha was distracted by all the preparations that had to be made. She came to Him and asked, "Lord, don't You care that my sister has left me to do the work by myself? Tell her to help me!"

"Martha, Martha," the Lord answered, "you are worried and upset about many things, but only one thing is needed. Mary has chosen what is better, and it will not be taken away from her." (Luke 10:38–42)

What do we see at that window?

The disciples are with Jesus initially, but they don't appear to be with Him now. Why? Is the house too small? Do they all need a break from each other after being on the road for so long?

Is Jesus tired, is that why He comes to this house?

Is He hungry? If so, for what? For food? Or is He hungry for something else, something that maybe the crowds and His disciples can't give Him?

Jesus is on the way to Jerusalem, on the way to His death. A few miles before He gets there, He stops here, at the home of these two women. He stops here, I think, because He is hungry for someone who will listen, someone who will understand, someone who will feel something of the heaviness He carries with Him on that uphill road to Jerusalem. Yes, He is hungry. But not for food.

Which of these hungers does Martha see when she greets Him at the door? Does she see a window into what is going on inside Him, a window into what He is thinking, feeling, needing? Or does she see just the leanness in His face and the angle of the sun, telling her it's nearly time for dinner?

Martha goes to the kitchen to prepare that dinner, leaving Mary sitting at Jesus' feet. What words is He aching to say, not just to Mary but to both of them? What words is He aching to hear, not just from Mary but from both of them?

Only one of them, though, pauses at that window. Only one of them sees the hunger in His soul. And it's not Martha.

Martha's in the kitchen. She works faster to make up for Mary's absence, but the faster she works the more steamed-up she gets. Finally she wipes the sweat from her face and storms out of the kitchen with a frying-pan-of-a-question waving in her hand. But why does she shake it at Jesus and not at Mary? And why does she refer to her as "my sister" instead of by name? The answers to those questions reveal something not only of her frustration but her anger.

Can you hear in her question not just the irritation but the indictment? "Lord, don't you care?" Instead of waiting for an answer, Martha issues an order. What does that tell you about the nature of her question and about the tone of voice she used in asking it?

But her wrath is met with a gentle answer. There is great tenderness in Jesus' reply. Can you hear it?

In the past I have more or less identified with Mary. But over the years, as I have had the opportunity to look deeper into my life, the more I see of Martha. The truth, I think, is that there is something of both sisters in all of us. And that is why so many of us so much of the time find ourselves in the middle of an inner tug-of-war, pulled one way by our duties and another by our devotion.

The words spoken to Martha are words spoken also to the Martha in me. But what were those words correcting? It was her worry, not her work. It was her being upset, not her being under pressure. The issue wasn't her preparations; it was her distractions. It wasn't the many things; it was that the many things didn't revolve around the one thing that was needed.

There was no quiet center that Martha was working from, no solitude of heart, no still axis around which her activities revolved. That's why the wheels fell off her attitude. And that's why, with some regularity, they fall off of mine.

When my attitude starts to wobble, I know it's because I'm distracted. I don't realize how much I'm distracted, though, until the axis starts grinding and heating up. Like Martha, I get frustrated, irritated, and sometimes stomping-mad-tell-somebody-off angry.

I know a wheel is starting to fall off when the meal I'm preparing becomes more important than the people I'm preparing it for. When my work becomes more important than the family I'm working for. When a point I'm making becomes more important than the person I'm making it to. That's how I can I tell I've lost the still axis. When I lose sight of what's more important. When I lose a sense of the sacredness of another human being, especially the human beings closest to me, the ones in my family.

I want to live in a way so that I don't lose sight of what's important or lose a sense of the sacredness of others. I want to live in a way so I can see windows of the soul.

I don't want to live in the kitchen of religious activity, distracted with all my preparations. I don't want to live slumped over some steamed-up stove, worried and upset about so many things. I want to live at the Savior's feet, gazing into His eyes, listening to His words, and seeing as many windows as He'll show me.

At His feet is where we learn to pause at those windows. It starts by loving Him and longing to hear His voice. When we're slaving away in some kitchen where the pots and pans are clanging, it's hard to hear that voice. But when we're at His feet and our heart is still, we can hear Him even when He whispers.

A Prayer for Solitude

Help me, O God,

To be a still axis in the wheel of activities that revolves around my life.
Deliver me from my distractions, which are many,
*   and lead me to a quiet place of devotion at Your feet.*
Teach me there how to pause at more windows.
I know I won't see everything,
*   but help me see something.*
So much passes me by
*   without attention, let alone, appreciation;*
*   without reflection, let alone, reverence;*
*   without thought, let alone, thankfulness.*
Slow me down, Lord, so I may see the windows in roller rinks
*   and the overarching grandeur of Your image*
*   in the Sistine Chapel of the soul . . .*

Something in the Window

Earth's crammed with heaven,
And every common bush afire with God;
But only he who sees takes off his shoes;
The rest sit round it and pluck blackberries.

ELIZABETH BARRETT BROWNING
Aurora Leigh

When we stand before a common bush, is there anything more to see than blackberries? Twig and root, leaf and fruit, is that all there is?

Or is there something more?

When we look at a work of art, we know there is something there more than paint, but is there something more than picture? When we listen to music, we know there is something there more than notes, but is there something more than song? When we read a book, we know there is something there more than words, but is there something more than story?

Is there something more than what we see on the surface?

"Art is at once surface and symbol," said Oscar Wilde in the preface to his haunting story, *The Picture of Dorian Gray*. Wilde's story is a Faustian tale in which the central character relinquishes his soul to retain his youthful good looks. A full-length portrait is made of him by an older artist named Hallward, and although Dorian doesn't age over the years, his portrait does. With each cruel word and evil deed, the portrait chronicles the decay of his soul. The hair turns stringy and gray. The eyes grow cold and cunning. The mouth becomes twisted and wrinkled.

One night the artist confronts Dorian with the rumored accusations he has heard.

> "Your name was implicated in the most terrible confession I ever read. I told him that it was absurd—that I knew you thoroughly, and that you were incapable of anything of this kind. Know you? I wonder do I know you? Before I could answer that, I would have to see your soul."
>
> "To see my soul!" muttered Dorian Gray, starting up from the sofa and turning almost white from fear.
>
> "Yes," answered Hallward, gravely, and with deep-toned sorrow in has voice—"to see your soul. But only God can do that."
>
> A bitter laugh of mockery broke from the lips of the younger man. "You shall see it yourself, tonight!" he cried, seizing a lamp from the table. "Come: it is your own handiwork. Why shouldn't you look at it?"

Dorian shows him the portrait, and the artist is horrified. By the end of the story, though, it is Dorian who is horrified. He can't escape the picture or its mute accusations that testify against him. Trapped in his anguish, he lashes out at the artist and murders him. The night he returns from the murder, he yanks the veil from the portrait and sees blood dripping from the portrait's hands.

The sight terrifies him, for the grotesque image was not a picture but a window, allowing him to see what only God could truly see—his soul.

"You use the arts to see your soul," said the playwright George Bernard Shaw. But we also use the arts to see something else—the soul of the artist.

If we stand before a van Gogh, for example, and see only the brilliance of his colors, we have not seen van Gogh, only the palette from which he worked. If we see only sunflowers and starry nights and the sad people in his pictures, we have seen more than colors, but we haven't seen van Gogh. If, on the other hand, we sense in those pictures a passionate search for God and a compassionate reach for people, we have seen the artist. We have seen through the paint and the picture to glimpse something of his soul.

The soul, though at all times hidden, is at all times revealed, expressing itself through everything we say and do. Through the ordinary brushstrokes of our everyday life, a portrait of our soul is being painted.

I am thinking about the portrait of the woman I love.

Somewhere between "Dear Ken" and "Love, Judy" something of her soul is expressed through the notes she has written me. Something of her soul is made audible through her laughter, which fills our house like music. Something of her soul is made visible through the colors she has chosen to decorate that house, which are warm and inviting, through the type of furniture, which is casual and comfortable, even the way she has arranged the furniture reveals something of her desire to make all who live there and visit there feel welcome.

Arranged in the entryway is a children's table and chairs, though the children are too big now to use them. In cozy nooks are little teapots and teacups, an old doll in a doll buggy, all of which reveal something about her and the tender feelings she has for children. On the shelf is a book she wrote, a children's book. On the nightstand are the books she reads. All of these are elements of a larger picture.

The homemade rolls she serves at Thanksgiving that taste like hot buttered clouds and the melt-in-your-mouth caramels she makes at Christmas, all these reveal something about her love for her family and her desire to make the holidays a little more special, a little more memorable.

She tucks the kids in bed every night and double checks their math. With them she plays double-solitaire and with them she puts together puzzles and with them she sits at the end of their beds to help them put together the puzzle of their young lives, to help them pick which card they should play next in the solitary decisions that sometime or another in life we all have to make. All of these things, down to the most ordinary and everyday of them, is a window of her soul.

Something is in that window.

And when I pause to look, something like the morning sun streams into my soul and wakens me to everything in her that is beautiful and precious to God.

To see what is in those windows we first have to stop, and then, as C. S. Lewis advised, "we must look, and go on looking till we have certainly seen exactly what is there."

Solomon lived his life that way, looking to see exactly what was there in the everyday moments of his life. One of those moments is preserved for us in the book of Proverbs.

I went past the field of the sluggard,
*   past the vineyard of the man who lacks judgment;*
thorns had come up everywhere,
*   the ground was covered with weeds,*
*   and the stone wall was in ruins.*
I applied my heart to what I observed
*   and learned a lesson from what I saw:*

A little sleep, a little slumber,
  a little folding of the hands to rest—
and poverty will come on you like a bandit
  and scarcity like an armed man.

PROVERBS 24:30–34

Solomon sees thorns, weeds, and a broken-down wall. But through
them he sees something else. He sees the owner's soul, or at least a glimpse of it.

But having seen it, Solomon doesn't shake his head and walk away.
He stays. He keeps looking. And through the tangled overgrowth he spots a
parable: Casual neglect leads to catastrophic loss. He gleans something from
this individual field that applies to whatever field is under our care, whether
it's a backyard row of tomatoes or a budding family or a burgeoning business.

How many people, I wonder, passed that field without looking?
How many glanced over their shoulder but didn't stop? How many stopped
but didn't see anything beyond the overgrowth? How many saw beyond the
overgrowth to the negligence of the owner but never gained from it wisdom
for their own lives?

There is something beyond the surface of the everyday events of
our lives and something beyond the surface of the lives of the everyday people
we pass by. Sometime or another we have all seen it, or at least sensed it. And
if we can't put our finger on it, it puts its finger on us, tapping us on the
shoulder, urging us to stop and look and listen to what God may be saying to
us through them.

God speaks through many things. The field of a sluggard and the
fruit of someone's life are just two of them.

How many times, though, have we passed those fields without
stopping to see what was there? How many times have we seen the fruit of
someone's labor but not the soul of the laborer? How many times have we
seen but not learned, watched but not wondered what lesson this person's life
could be teaching us?

How many times have we sat around plucking blackberries, thinking blackberries were all that was there? How many times have we failed to

see the heavenly blaze in the earthly bushes we brush by every day on our way to somewhere else? How many times have we failed to hear what was spoken to us there?

A story is told of a pagan who asked a rabbi, "Why did God speak to Moses from the thornbush?" For the pagan thought God should have spoken instead in a peal of thunder on the peak of some majestic mountain. The rabbi answered, "To teach you that there is no place on earth where God's glory is not, not even in a humble thornbush."

Can we see the divine humility in the way that word of God was spoken? Can we see the even greater humility when the word of God was spoken in the middle of the night through the splayed legs of a teenage girl in the barnyard stench of a stable, where divine eloquence was reduced to the whimper of a child?

But why was the word of God so spoken? Why then? Why there? Why in that way?

To teach us, I think, that there is no time, no place, no event so earthly that God cannot be there, speaking through them. These moments where earth is crammed with heaven, these Bethlehem moments where something divine is birthed through very human wombs, will go unnoticed unless we realize the meek and unassuming way that God characteristically comes.

If we are to see the divine artist's soul mediated through the lesser things of flesh and blood, field and stream, flute and drum, we must look for windows in places we are unaccustomed to looking, in small towns and in stables. We must listen for voices we are unaccustomed to hearing, a star in the sky saying, "Come this way," or a dream in the night saying, "Go another way." We must look in those windows and go on looking until we see something sacred in the straw.

A Prayer for Transcendence

Thank You, God,

For Your hand that reaches to me,
touching my arm, tapping my shoulder,
telling me to pause and to look and to listen
at all the windows of the soul.
Help me to see something in those windows,
something of heaven in every earthly event,
something of the divine spark in every human soul.
Please, dear God, give me grace to stand, shoes in hand,
before all that in some way bears Your glory,
for I don't want to spend my days
just sitting around
plucking blackberries . . .

Longings of the Soul

There have been times when I think we do not desire heaven; but more often I find myself wondering whether, in our heart of hearts, we have ever desired anything else.

C. S. LEWIS
The Problem of Pain

In J. R. R. Tolkien's *The Hobbit*, the magician Gandalf told the reluctant and unlikely hero Bilbo Baggins, "There is more to you than you know." He said this, knowing that within the hobbit's veins coursed blood not only from the sedentary Baggins side of the family but also from the swashbuckling Took side. We have a similar mingling of blood within us from a lineage that is both human and divine.

Within us the dust of the earth and the breath of heaven are joined in a mysterious union only death can separate. But that relationship is often a strained one, for while the body is fitted for a terrestrial environment—with lungs to breathe air and teeth to chew food and feet to walk on dirt—the soul is extraterrestrial, fitted for heaven. It breathes other air, eats other food, walks other terrain.

Most of the time, though, we are burrowed away in our hobbit holes and don't give a thought to our heritage.

Bilbo Baggins certainly didn't. Not until Gandalf entered his life. The magician entered his life through the front door of the hobbit's burrow. Before the door shut, a dozen motley dwarfs followed on his heels, and on the turn of its hinges, the quiet world of Bilbo Baggins dramatically changed.

Suddenly he found himself saddled with the unwanted responsibility of hosting a houseful of strangers. After emptying his pantry to satisfy their ravenous appetites, the exhausted Bilbo plopped on the hearth of his fireplace before a crackling fire. As he rested there, the dwarfs joined in singing an ancient song, and as he listened, "something Tookish woke up inside him, and he wished to go and see the great mountains, and hear the pine-trees and the waterfalls, and explore the caves, and wear a sword instead of a walking stick."

Whenever I hear Górecki's "Third Symphony" or Rachmaninoff's "Vespers," whenever I read Rilke's poem "The Man Watching" or Harper Lee's book *To Kill a Mockingbird*, whenever I see the movie *Camelot* or the stage play *Les Miserables*, something "Tookish" wakes in me, a sleepy-eyed awareness that there is more to me than I know. And suddenly I want to set aside my walking stick and strap on a sword, and leave the cozy security of my hobbit hole in search of some far-off adventure.

Like the dormant gene that wakes with the dawn of our adolescence, rousing us toward adulthood, moments like these reveal we are destined for greater things than make-believe adventures in the fenced-in yards of our youth.

Art, literature, and music waken us to the alluring beauty of that destiny. But, as C. S. Lewis cautions, "The book or the music in which we thought the beauty was located will betray us if we trust to them; it was not *in* them, it only came through them, and what came *through* them was longing. . . . They are not the thing itself; they are only the scent of a flower we have not found, the echo of a tune we have not heard, news from a country we have never visited."

The Baggins part of me, though, wants nothing of all this. It wants to sit in its hobbit hole, safe and snug, with an inside latch locking out the dangers and uncertainties of the world beyond its door. Another part of me, though, wants something more. To see more. To hear more. To explore more.

To be more.

We live in a constant tension between those two parts, the lofty side of our nature and the lowly side. Like a tree, we are torn between two worlds, a part of us rooted in the soil, another part reaching for the sky.

But because our roots can grasp soil more securely than our leaves can grasp sky, the soil seems more real. It is something we can see and hold in our hand. But heaven, heaven escapes our grasp. We can't hold it any more than a leaf can hold sky.

Yet something of the sky is taken into its pores, and something of the sun is taken into its cells. That is how it receives the carbon dioxide and makes the chlorophyll it needs to live. If the tree is deprived of all the sky has to offer, it will wither, putting more pressure on the roots to provide its nourishment. In the same way, if the soul is somehow shut off from God, shielded from the sunshine of its eternal significance, it will seek significance elsewhere, sending out its roots in search of the right job, the right school, the right organizations to join, burrowing deeper, thinking if it gets enough money, enough power, enough prestige, it will satisfy its longing for significance.

This longing is an essential function of the soul. In this respect the soul is closer to the stomach than to any other of the body's organs. When the pancreas is functioning properly, for example, it does not draw attention to itself. The stomach does. When we need something to eat or drink, the stomach signals us through hunger or thirst. If we neglect these longings, the louder and more insistent they become. If we neglect them long enough, these longings will consume us.

Before they get to that point, though, we usually reach for something to take the edge off the hunger. When it's a candy bar we reach for, the consequences aren't critical. But when those longings are sexual, how we go about satisfying them becomes very critical. "Stolen water is sweet; food eaten in secret is delicious!" said Solomon, who went on to say, in essence, that if we reach into the wrong cupboards to sate that hunger or into the wrong wells to satisfy that thirst, it will destroy us.

The same is true of our spiritual longings. "My soul thirsts for you," cried David, "my body longs for you, in a dry and weary land where there is no water." Our longings for God may not be as ravenous as David's, but they are as real. Because the hunger hurts, though, we try to take the edge off it in any way we can. One of those ways is with religious activity. And that can include the activity of reading books, listening to tapes, or going to seminars. Through these things, which are often very good things, even nourishing things, we are fed the experiences of others. But they are not *our* experiences. I can read a psalm about David crying out from a cave in the wilderness, and I should read that psalm, but it is not *my* psalm. It is not my psalm because it is not my cave, not my wilderness, and not my tears.

For so long in my life I expected my experience of God to be like one of those psalms, structured with pleasing rhythms, full of poetic images, a thing of beauty and grace. What I learned is that those psalms were born out of great hunger—a hunger that no food on this earth can satisfy.

"He who is satisfied has never truly craved," said Abraham Heschel, and he said this, I think, because he knew that heaven's richest food does not satisfy our longings but rather intensifies them.

True food from heaven, food placed for us on the windowsills of the soul, is like the Turkish Delight in C. S. Lewis' children's book, *The Lion, the Witch, and the Wardrobe*. In it the Queen of Narnia entices one of the children, named Edmund, with a magical food called Turkish Delight. It was sweet to the taste and light on the stomach and more delicious than anything he had ever tasted. But here was the magic. The more Edmund ate, the more he wanted to eat, until his appetite became insatiable, and he would do anything for another taste.

The food offered Edmund is similar to the food offered us at the windows of the soul only in this respect. The more we taste, the more we long for another taste. And another. Until at last the hunger grows so intense it transforms not only our lesser longings but our very lives themselves.

This longing that wells up in us, though, does not spring into existence on its own. "God is always previous," is the way the theologian von Hügel put it. "You would not have called to me unless I had been calling to you," is the way Aslan put it, the lion in the Narnia Chronicles who called Edmund and three other children from England into the magical land of Narnia. The way the apostle John put it was, "We love because he first loved us."

Maybe, too, that is why we long.

"God's yearning for us stirs up our longing in response," said Howard Macy in *Rhythms of the Inner Life*. "God's initiating presence may be ever so subtle—an inward tug of desire, a more-than-coincidence meeting of words and events, a glimpse of the beyond in a storm or in a flower—but it is enough to make the heart skip a beat and to make us want to know more."

And it is enough to make us leave behind our walking stick, strap on a sword, and search for that flower whose scent is so enticing, for that music whose echo is so enchanting, and for that far-off country whose news seems too good to be true . . .

. . . but is.

A *Prayer for* Nourishment

How inarticulate are the longings of my soul, O God,
yet how acute are its pangs.
How incapable am I in understanding those longings,
let alone, in tending them.
Feed me with food, O God, that will best nourish my soul,
food that will intensify rather than satisfy
my love for You
and my longing to be with You.
Awaken every eternal seed You have planted in my soul
so while I am yet rooted in this earth
something of heaven might blossom in my life . . .

Opening the Window

Man's walled mind has no access to a ladder upon which he can, of his own strength, rise to knowledge of God. Yet his soul is endowed with translucent windows that open to the beyond.

ABRAHAM HESCHEL
God in Search of Man: A Philosophy of Judaism

Michelangelo's painting on the ceiling of the Sistine Chapel, the one in which God is reaching His hand to Adam's, their fingers not quite touching, symbolizes God's relationship to all humanity for all of human history. Whenever He succeeds in reaching us, a window opens between heaven and earth in a moment of revelation.

What we are offered at those moments of revelation is something so much more tantalizing than Turkish Delight. We are offered words from God. Words of grace and love. Words of guidance and correction. Words of wisdom and understanding. Words of forgiveness and assurance.

Words that our soul hungers for.

"Man shall not live by bread alone," Jesus said, "but by every word that proceeds from the mouth of God." If this is true, our very lives depend on those words. They are, in fact, the daily bread of our soul. But what are those words? And where do we find them?

Through the prophet Isaiah, God provides a clue: "As the rain and the snow come down from heaven, and do not return to it without watering the earth and making it bud and flourish, so that it yields seed for the sower and bread for the eater, so is my word that goes out from my mouth: It will not return to me empty, but will accomplish what I desire and achieve the purpose for which I sent it."

Many have understood this passage as a reference to the Scriptures, thinking if a verse is quoted in conversation, or if a pamphlet of verses is put in a sack lunch for the homeless, or if a Bible is put into the hands of a skeptic, fruit will come of it. Often, though, our experience proves otherwise. The passage, in fact, suggests otherwise.

Look deeper into the analogy. It compares the word that goes out of God's mouth to the rain and snow that go out of the sky. When rain or snow falls to the ground, it trickles into streams, pools into lakes, filters into subterranean wells. Dip your hand in a lake, and there is rain channeled from the mountains and snow melted from its peaks. Dig a well, and there also is something of the rain. Peer into the stem of a honeysuckle, and there a nectared tear wept by the rain. Crush a leaf, and out comes a drop of what was once rain. Bite into a peach, and there is something of the winter snow mingled with spring showers in its succulent juices. Even in the desert, where there seems no trace of moisture, you can cut open a saguaro cactus and find something of the rain reservoired inside.

Like rain and snow, the word of God permeates the earth. To say God's word can be found only in certain places, like the Bible, for example, is to say, in effect, that rain water can be found only in lakes where it is most visible. But everywhere we look there are traces of His word. In history. In the circumstances of our lives. In every nook of humanity and every crannied flower of creation.

If God created the world with words that went forth from His mouth, words like "Let there be lights in the expanse of the sky to separate the day from the night, and let them serve as signs to mark seasons and days and years," it follows that the sun and moon and stars are echoes of those words and that something of the divine mind and its purposes can be understood in studying them. If we look with the right eyes, listen with the right ears, we will understand the natural creation as a form of sign language through which God expresses Himself.

If aeons ago God spoke judgment on the world through an inundating sermon of water, then the geological strata form the sedimentary pages where those words are recorded.

If the word of God went forth and became flesh and dwelt among us, then every word and every deed of the life of Christ became the vocabulary through which God spoke to the world, and through which He speaks to it still.

If the word of God dwells within us, then God speaks to others, however inarticulately, through the language of our life.

If God says yes in answer to our prayers, then the circumstances that constitute that answer are echoes of the yes He has spoken. Most often those answers come to us by way of a messenger. That messenger may be an angel or a work of art, a prophet or a person we met for lunch, a Scripture or a song, a vision or a dream, a scene from nature or from a night at the movies. Just as the rain and snow do not cycle back to the atmosphere without first accomplishing their work on earth, so these messengers do not return to God empty-handed without accomplishing the purpose for which they were sent.

Something of His word has also been written in our soul. Not just the moral law written on the tablets of our heart, although that too. But something like the genealogy of Christ recorded in Luke's gospel, which traces the Messiah's lineage, not back to Abraham as Matthew's genealogy does, but all the way back to God Himself. We have within us a genetic memory, so to speak, of such a lineage.

Like any memory, it can be repressed, but it cannot be erased. Something has been written in the depths of our being, something the soul strains to recall, words inscribed by the very hand of God, inky recollections of our origins, telling us we are more than a mere collection of chemical reactions or animal instincts.

Jesus tried to tell us that when He answered the question posed to Him regarding whether or not we should pay taxes. He had someone in the crowd examine a coin and then asked, "Whose portrait is this? And whose inscription?" When the reply was "Caesar's," Jesus said, "Give to Caesar what is Caesar's, and to God what is God's." The inference we can draw from his illustration is that we, like the coin, bear the portrait and inscription of our sovereign. We bear within our soul the very image of God, stamped with His likeness, with the inscription that we belong to Him. The coin can be defaced or devalued, but its origin and ownership are indisputable.

Indeed, there is more to us than we know.

At times like this, Jesus spoke in plain language. Other times, though, He spoke in parables, which is how I think God most often speaks to us. He speaks to us in parables through nature, uses the language of parable in history and in dreams and in the circumstances of our lives.

Sometimes those circumstances come together in such an extraordinary set of coincidences it catches our attention. What we see in those circumstances are pieces of a puzzle we are invited to put together. The longer we stare at the individual pieces, the more connections we see. Colors match, shapes interlock, and before long a picture emerges. Just like working with a jigsaw puzzle, one moment we see only irregular shapes of green, the next moment we see grass; one moment we see only disconnected shards of blue, the next moment we see sky.

Parables are pictures that emerge from the jigsaw events of life, however irregular or disconnected they may first appear. "All happenings, great and small, are parables whereby God speaks," said Malcolm Muggeridge; "the art of life is to get the message." To see all that is offered us at the windows of the soul and to reach out and receive what is offered, this is the art of living.

But it is an art and not a science, and so it is not as exact as most of us would prefer. There is room for error. Which makes us uncomfortable. But because it's not all black and white but more like shadows cast by the substance of things unseen, there is also room for faith.

But there is a danger, even for the faithful.

The natural tendency is to analyze such moments of grace, formulize them into principles so the moment can be recreated, and then legalize the principles into codes of conduct as a measure of spirituality. In doing so, we take not only the spontaneity out of our relationship with God but also the vitality.

God, though, will not allow Himself to be confined like a genie in a lamp. Neither will He allow Himself to be controlled as a genie is controlled by the holder of the lamp, summoned at the will of the one who knows just where to rub and how often. It is God who opens the window, not us. All we can do is receive, or not receive, what is offered there.

Because the soul belongs to the unseen realm, whenever we speak of it, we have to feel our way in the dark, groping for words as we explore its mysteries by the dim light of our own understanding.

My own understanding is that of a writer, not a theologian. But if faith is the substance of things unseen, maybe we come closer to spiritual things with our imaginations than our intellects. Maybe analysis cannot probe as deeply into such things as can art. If so, the artist, the musician, the writer, may have the upper hand, however feeble, when it comes to such things.

As a writer, I work with words and not numbers, with images and not equations. Because of that, it is likely I won't get it just right, that the sum of my thinking will be, at best, an approximation.

What I offer in the following chapters are little more than scratch-paper estimates of how I think a person hears from God. In them are some of the echoes I have heard or thought I have heard, and some of the glimpses I have seen or thought I have seen, at some of the windows of the soul I have encountered on my own spiritual journey.

Reduced to their lowest common denominator, they are little more than something of my experience with hunger and something of my experience with being fed. As you walk with me through these experiences, I hope most of what you read makes sense and that some of it makes a difference in your own experience with God.

A Prayer for Grace

Thank You, God,

For those moments in my life
  when You opened a window
    and offered a word
      that nourished the hunger in my soul.
Give me the grace to realize
  that these are the words I live by,
    not by bread alone,
      whatever form that bread may take
        however satisfying it may seem at the time.
Give me the grace to live not just reflectively but receptively,
  that I may not only notice when a window is opened
    but also receive what is offered,
      understanding that what is offered
        is my soul's daily bread . . .

Part Two

Windows of Vocation

There is always one moment in childhood when the door opens and lets in the future.

GRAHAM GREENE
The Power and the Glory

While in seminary, I sometimes heard students and professors talk about their "calling." Called to teach. Called to the mission field. Called to pastor. It struck me at the time as kind of a small-town colloquialism. The kind of talk you would hear at some tent-revival on the littered edge of town. The church in which I had been raised didn't talk like that. It didn't do altar calls. What it did was all very private and hushed and liturgically restrained. If you were called at all, it was by someone on the phone committee.

And yet, I sensed a calling on my life. That's how I ended up in seminary. But it was not the specific calling that I heard some of the people at seminary talking about. For me it came in a more general way.

It came the summer after my senior year in high school when I was at a Young Life camp in Colorado. During a twenty-minute time of silence after one of the evening messages, I felt compelled to answer Christ's love as it called to me from the cross. That night, while sitting under a tree, I answered that call with my life, thinking my life would be of little use to Him, but still, if He wanted it for something, it was His for the taking.

Answering that call seemed so natural. So much had been given; so little had been asked in return. How could I not entrust my life to so great a love? And yet somewhere in the subterranean places of my heart flowed a very quiet but very real fear of trusting too much. I feared that if I got too serious about my relationship with God, that if I got close enough to where He could see the whites of my eyes, He might call me out from the crowd, call me by name, send me somewhere I didn't want to go. I remembered the Sunday school stories. We didn't have altar calls, but we had Sunday school. I remembered where He sent Jonah. And that thing about the storm. And that sloshing ordeal in the belly of the whale. That could be me if I wasn't careful how I worded things. He might send me to Ninevah.

I remembered the story of Abraham too. "The friend of God," is how he was described, and look where that got him. What if God asked me to take a knife to all the Isaacs in my life? You get on a first-name basis with God and who knows what could happen to you?

Of course, that wasn't the theme of the Sunday school lesson, but it was a real, however quiet, theme that ran through my life.

I feared that God would call me to the place I least wanted to go. Africa. And that He would call me to the work I least wanted to do. Missionary work. Hacking through a jungle with a machete, swatting at mosquitoes in the sweltering heat, dodging poison darts. I remembered the Tarzan movies. I remembered them better than the Sunday school stories. "Bwana, look out! Simba!" I remembered the lions and the alligators and the boa constrictors that squeezed the life from your body and swallowed you whole. And did you see the episode with the quicksand?

Anywhere, God. Anywhere but Africa.

As it turned out, or should I say, as it has turned out so far, He has not called me to Africa. But He has called other people there. And other people answered that call with their lives. One of them was Albert Schweitzer.

The call came in his childhood.

One day when he and his family went to Colmar, France, they came to the town square and stood before a monument to General Bruat, sculpted by Bartholdi, the sculptor of the Statue of Liberty. But it was not the mighty general that caught young Albert's eye.

At the base of the statue were four smaller figures, one at each corner. One of them was an African enslaved in chains. His nearly naked body, rippling with strength, sat with its head angled to the ground and its eyes fixed in a melancholy stare.

That moment made an indelible impression on Schweitzer. In his book *Memories of Childhood and Youth,* he described the figure and the impact it made. "It is a figure of Herculean proportions, but the face wears an expression of thoughtful sadness which I could not forget, and every time we went to Colmar I tried to find the time to go and look for it. The countenance spoke to me of the misery of the Dark Continent, and even today I make a pilgrimage to it when I am in Colmar."

As he grew up, Schweitzer prayed for the suffering in the world, which this statue reminded him of. Even in childhood, he believed that the good and happy life he had was a gift, and he felt a sense of indebtedness for having received it.

Such thoughts flew in lazy circles in Schweitzer's mind as he was enjoying the cozy solitude of an Easter vacation one spring day in 1886. The ascending sun angled in from a window in his room, as he lay in bed, half-awake, basking in the serenity of early morning. And then, as auspiciously as a sparrow landing on his windowsill, his destiny fluttered into view.

"I awoke with the thought," he later recounted, "that my good fortune was not to be taken as something self-evident. . . . In peaceful reflection, while the birds were singing, I decided before I got up that I would be justified in devoting myself until I was thirty to science and art in order to give myself thereafter to direct services to humanity."

In the years that followed, he gained doctorates in music, religion, and philosophy. But though his calling was clear, the specifics of that calling were not.

Until another morning.

It was an autumn morning in 1904, when his eye caught the green cover of a magazine lying on his writing desk. The magazine was the monthly report of the Paris Missionary Society, and the article his eyes fell on was titled, "The Needs of the Congo Mission." He sat down and read the article, which ended with the words, "Men who can say, at a sign from the King, 'Master, I go forth,' that is what the Church needs."

When he finished reading, his search was over. To him it was clear that his calling was to Africa. He felt compelled to go. But not as a missionary. As a physician. He spent the next nine years getting a doctorate in medicine. The last fifty-two years he served in a small hospital he had erected in the jungles of French Equatorial Africa, where he helped thousands and inspired millions.

For Schweitzer, his calling first came through a window in his childhood, a window he saw in a European town square that looked out over all of Africa. At another window on a spring day in 1886, that calling became clearer. And finally, at a window that opened one autumn day in 1904, it was as clear as the morning sun.

When I look back on my own life, there were windows in my childhood too, and all along the way into my adulthood.

Growing up, I had a gregarious father who was a great storyteller. I was not. I was a listener. I was the quiet, red-headed kid with a burr haircut who spent mornings tunneling in the backyard, building forts while defending the Alamo or refighting World War II. Afternoons I went padding off in my bare feet and cutoffs with my little red wagon in tow, collecting everything from Coke bottles to fossils to horned toads. Evenings I caught lightning bugs in jars and played hide-and-seek in the neighborhood.

All the while, the seeds of stories were being planted in my mind. But those seeds took years to germinate. They lay in the fallow fields of my memory as the school years passed like seasons, grade school gradually giving way to junior high, junior high to high school, and high school to college.

After my first year in college, I felt drawn to seminary. "Called" would be too strong a word. What was it that drew me? Admiration for the faculty? Certainly that played a part. My friends, almost all of whom were going to seminary? Undoubtedly that was a factor. Insecurity? Thinking a seminary education would give me the answers I didn't have, the academic agility to squeeze out of a theological corner someone had backed me into? All of these things, I'm sure, played a part in drawing me to seminary. A sense of calling did not.

While in seminary, I thought I wanted to teach in a state university, something in English, the Bible as literature, maybe, something like that, with summers off to write, though about what, I hardly knew at the time.

As I began making applications, I realized, suddenly and dishearteningly after four hard years, that my degree from seminary was the wrong key to open the doors of a state institution. During that time I was asked to start a rural church just outside of my hometown of Fort Worth, Texas. For two years I pastored by Braille mostly, feeling my way in the dark, getting ready for Sunday when this shy kid would go on display as the center of everyone's attention.

But God had not called me to be a pastor. Other people had. Other people thought it would be a good opportunity for me, an offer I shouldn't turn down. After all, I wasn't getting any other offers. None of the universities were calling. It was the type of thing people thought I would be good at, and being the type of person that wanted to please people, I took the job. Not the only reason I took it, of course, but certainly one of them.

After two years of this awkwardness, I felt something like "the call of the wild" compelling me to write. It was then I wrote my first book, a short novel for children. I woke each day with an excitement I didn't have as a pastor. I threw myself into each day, each sentence, each page. At the end of the day, even on the days that went past midnight, I had energy left over. And when I woke up the next morning, I woke up refreshed, eager to get at the next chapter. It was all so satisfying, so fulfilling, so, so . . . so fun.

And I felt guilty about that. Not guilty for enjoying writing so much—Guilty for enjoying pastoring so little.

When I finished the book, it was like finding the missing piece to the jigsaw puzzle of my life. Suddenly everything fit, everything made sense. I knew then that God had crafted my personality, shaped my life experiences, and given me certain skills to make a writer out of me. Was this "call of the wild" the call of God? Could something that made me feel this good, this fulfilled, this whole, be God's calling?

Those two months it took me to write that book were like a window full of sunshine and fresh air, a window with a songbird on the sill, calling my name.

Now, as I look back on my life, I can see the windows that framed my vocation, starting as far back as the fourth grade. I remember coming in from recess, and our teacher Miss Kobel reading to us as we rested our sweating heads on our worn, oak desks. She was tall and lanky, and with her short dark hair and lean angular face, she reminded me of the picture of Abraham Lincoln hanging on the classroom wall.

She had a deep, resonant voice, which she used in reading us *Charlotte's Web*. Her voice wove E. B. White's words into a magic carpet that transported me from that hot, Texas classroom to breezy country farms and county fairs where a spider named Charlotte saved the life of a runt pig named Wilbur. I still remember the words she embroidered in her web to help save him. SOME PIG. TERRIFIC. HUMBLE.

And I still remember the feeling that washed over me when Miss Kobel read the last paragraph: "Wilbur never forgot Charlotte. Although he loved her children and her grandchildren dearly, none of the new spiders ever quite took her place in his heart. She was in a class by herself. It is not often that someone comes along who is a true friend and a good writer. Charlotte was both."

"There is always one moment in childhood," said the novelist Graham Green, "when the door opens and lets the future in." For me, that day was a school day after recess as I rested my head on my wooden desk and listened to Miss Kobel reading *Charlotte's Web*.

That moment, as I look back on it after all these years, showed me something about myself and was a window that looked out onto my vocation. Was it a coincidence that the first book I wrote was a children's book?

I don't think so.

As I look back, I see other windows in my life, windows that hinted at who I was and what I should be doing with my life. If anybody asked me what I liked about school when I was young, I answered as I suppose all kids answered then and answer still: recess. And if asked what besides recess I liked about school: lunch. The truth was, what I loved most was when our teacher read to us.

And something else. But I had to dig through my old toy box to find out what.

Little has survived my childhood. A few soldiers from a Fort Apache set, a few from the Alamo, the Civil War, World War II. Some marbles. A stamp collection. Slingshot. A stuffed tiger I slept with, threadbarely surviving the molt of the years. And amid a tatterdemalion of report cards and schoolwork, there survives a social studies notebook on the Orient.

When I came across the old notebook, I took a few minutes to thumb through it. I remember, maybe for the first time since childhood, how I loved putting together those notebooks. I loved designing a creative cover, drawing maps with colored pencils and shading the borders. I loved writing reports. The cursive penmanship was a source of delight for me. Even the fluid blue of fountain pen ink somehow gave me pleasure. I loved sketching illustrations and cutting out pictures from magazines to use in the notebook. The whole creative process brought me joy, holding the finished notebook in my hand, thumbing through it one last time before I turned it in.

On the back page of the notebook I noticed a comment by my teacher saying she had never had a student do such beautiful notebooks. The words made me pause. I had not remembered them. Back then I was too busy with baseball and four-square and dodge ball, and words like "beautiful" would have caused my face to scrunch up. But now, decades later as I look back at them, my face doesn't scrunch up, and the words seem to be saying something besides a teacher's kind commentary.

Look over here, they seem to be saying, *look in this window. It is a window into your soul. It is showing you something of who you are, what you love, and what you will be doing with your life if you listen to what your life is saying, where it is calling you.*

I look back on my youth and see reminders of who I was and hints of who I was to become. I see backyard forts and baseball mitts. I see cigar boxes that housed bug collections, Coke bottles rattling around in a red wagon, a bike with playing cards clothes-pinned to its spokes. I see a boy with a safety-pinned towel around his neck, running through the neighborhood, arms stretched before him, towel unfurling behind him. And I hear a narrator saying, "faster than a speeding bullet, more powerful than a locomotive." And I see neighbors throwing open their windows, wondering: "Is it a bird? Is it a plane?" And someone shouting: "It's Superman!"

But there are other things I remember from my childhood. Stacks of comic books I read by flashlight under my covers. A shelf of dog-eared Hardy Boy mysteries. The River Oaks Public Library where I was dropped off on Saturdays and lazy summer afternoons. Social studies notebooks on the Orient and other faraway lands. A diary I kept as a Boy Scout on a canoe trip into the Canadian wilderness. One of the reasons I remember all of these things is because they all brought me such joy.

Look back on your life, as I looked back on mine, and put frames around the things that brought you joy. Do you see the pictures? Look at them. Look closer. Deeper. Are they windows? If so, what is it you see in them? What is it you hear? A voice? What is that voice saying? And can you hear it above all the other voices that have called to you over the years?

"The voice we should listen to most as we choose a vocation," said Frederick Buechner in a graduation address, "is the voice that we might think we should listen to least, and that is the voice of our own gladness. What can we do that makes us the gladdest, what can we do that leaves us with the strongest sense of sailing true north and of peace, which is much of what gladness is? Is it making things with our hands out of wood or stone or paint or canvas? Or is it making something we hope like truth out of words? Or is it making people laugh or weep in a way that cleanses their spirit? I believe that if it is a thing that makes us truly glad, then it is a good thing and it is our thing and it is the calling voice that we were made to answer with our lives."

Seminary is a place where, of all places, I think, we should hear voices like that. I, for one, was too busy with school-work and supporting a family and ministry and trying to catch up on sleep to do much of that then. But now, as I look back, my greatest joy in seminary, what made me the gladdest, what left me with the strongest sense of sailing true north, was not poring over dusty volumes of theology or solving cryptic exegetical problems in Hebrew or Greek. It was not taking notes or taking tests or taking seats in chapel to hear the pantheon of speakers.

It was writing my master's thesis.

I was a writer, not a pastor. And if I had listened to my life, listened to the things that brought me joy, I would have known that. And I would have known it a long time ago, if only I had been looking.

We skip down the hallways of our youth, you and I, stopping now and then to catch our breath. And every now and then we catch something else. A glimpse of the future. *Our* future. A glimpse we caught when we came across a window suddenly flung open in front of us, its gossamer curtains lifted by a breeze redolent with the future, filling our lungs with refreshing air and our heart with hopeful dreams.

At that window we hear something like somebody calling our name, only in a language we can't quite understand, so we don't recognize who it is who is calling us or to where we are being called.

But we recognize the name.

Even in a foreign language, names translate closely to the original. Whoever it is calling us is calling us by our true name. Whispering to us a secret. Telling us who we are. And showing us what we will be doing with our lives if only we have the eyes to see, the ears to hear, and the faith to follow.

A Prayer for Joy

Help me, O God,

To listen to what it is that makes my heart glad
and to follow where it leads.
May joy, not guilt,
Your voice, not the voices of others,
Your will, not my willfulness,
be the guides that lead me to my vocation.
Help me to unearth the passions of my heart
that lay buried in my youth.
And help me to go over that ground again and again
until I can hold in my hands,
hold and treasure,
Your calling on my life . . .

Windows of Stories

What the storyteller is doing, of course, is looking through the windows of his imagination, trying to see things more clearly, hoping to help and enlighten and entertain others at the same time.

And sometimes, if the panes in the windows are clear, he does.

ARTHUR GORDON
Through Many Windows

Stories give us eyes other than our own with which to see the world. In Felix Salten's *Bambi*, for example, we are given the eyes of a newborn deer. Through them we see the wonder of his first encounter with a butterfly, which seemed to him as if it were a flower blown off its stem by the wind. Through those eyes we also see the terror of his first encounter with man entering the forest.

Stories can turn us into a boy, as Elie Wiesel's *Night* did, showing us through the eyes of a young teenager the horrors of the Holocaust. Or they can turn us into a girl, as Harper Lee's *To Kill a Mockingbird* did, showing us through the eyes of Scout Finch what it was like growing up in a small Alabama town in the 1930s.

Giving us other eyes, stories protect us from the small-town perils of our own parochial way of looking at things. They reveal something beyond the surface of other people's lives, other nation's lives, our own lives even.

The power of story is in the way it incarnates ideas, putting flesh and blood on skeletal principles. If you want to understand the dangers of ambition, for example, to understand it in a way that will impact you the rest of your life, read *The Thornbirds*. If you want to see the devastation of adultery in a way that will shake you, see the movie *Camelot*.

When we see such stories, with all their hardships, colors, and juices, they move us in ways that principles and prohibitions can't. They move us not by external forces but by internal ones. Not by law but by grace. By the quickening of our conscience and the stirrings of our heart.

In a moment of reflection Eugene Peterson once asked himself: "Who are the people who have made a difference in my life? Answer: The ones who weren't trying to make a difference."

For me, that person was Atticus Finch.

I grew up in Texas and lived there for the first thirty-six years of my life. I remember as a child seeing water fountains in department stores, labeled "White Only" and "Colored." I remember a black family coming to our church because the pastor of the church they attended asked them not to partake in Communion for fear it might split the church. Years later, in another church, I heard a man stand up and make a pronouncement that the first time a black person came through the door of the church, he was leaving. And one day, while doing research on a novel, I was scrolling through a reel of microfilm from newspapers of that post-war era and stopped at a photograph of a black man who had been lynched.

The men who lynched him were, I suspect, not much different from the men of Maycomb County in the book *To Kill a Mockingbird*. It's difficult to see how men could do such terrible things. Especially church-going, Bible-believing men. But they did.

Atticus Finch stood up to men like that.

He was the lawyer in Maycomb County who stood against the consensus of hometown opinion by defending a black man in court. He was a highly principled man, and if you've ever had a brush with someone highly principled, you know how prickly a brush like that can be. Atticus Finch wasn't like that. His principles were not lectured, they were lived. And one of the principles he lived, which he passed on to his children, was not to judge others till you walked around a while in their shoes.

In raising Jem and Scout, Atticus gave them those shoes. And the humility to try them on.

"What does the Lord require of you," asked Hosea, "but to do justice, love kindness, and walk humbly with your God?" Atticus Finch seems to me to have lived such a life. He was a man of courage and conviction, a man full of grace and truth, and in my mind a man a lot like Christ.

I have read only a few books on being a father; certainly I should have read more. Of the few I have read, I can recall only one or two of their titles and almost nothing of their contents. But Atticus Finch, he has stayed with me, that tall, lanky shadow of his falling across my path, ahead of me, straight and true.

He didn't tell me what a good father is supposed to be like; he showed me. How would Atticus handle this? What would *he* do? I would sometimes ask myself. And the times I answered that question with my life, I was a better father.

In the last scene of the story, Atticus is in Jem's room the night Bob Ewell vengefully broke the boy's arm and almost killed him. The final words of the story are spoken by Jem's sister Scout, as years later she recalled that night when Atticus waited up. "He would be there all night, and he would be there when Jem waked up in the morning."

It was what a father is supposed to do—to be there, watching over his children, all night if need be, and on into the morning.

When I finished the story, those words took on a life of their own, standing on the wooden porch of Atticus' house, lingering, staring back at me.

He would be there all night, and he would be there when Jem waked up in the morning.

And as I closed the book, the words followed me.

All the way home.

If a story is to follow us home, find entrance through some door of our heart, it must be asked, consciously or unconsciously, two questions:

What does this story have to say? And what does it have to say to me?

A few years ago when reading Norman Maclean's story *A River Runs Through It*, I wrestled with those questions. The opening paragraph establishes the central metaphor of the story with prose as fluid as a river. Listen as it ripples over and around the rocks of punctuation.

> In our family, there was no clear line between religion and fly fishing.
>
> We lived at the junction of great trout rivers in western Montana, and our father was a Presbyterian minister and a fly fisherman who tied his own flies and taught others. He told us about Christ's disciples being fishermen, and we were left to assume, as my brother and I did, that all first-class fishermen on the Sea of Galilee were fly fishermen and that John, the favorite, was a dry-fly fisherman.

The autobiographical story flowed with gentle ease, and although I didn't quite know where the story was going, it was pleasant just to float downstream on the soothing rhythm of the author's words. Not until the last three pages did the story open up for me, shortly after the point where the author's brother dies as an unsolved murder. Like a river turning a bend in the canyon of my mind, it revealed, suddenly and startlingly, this grand vista of human relationships. The vista opened up after a turn in the father's conversation with his surviving son.

"You like to tell true stories, don't you?" he asked, and I answered, "Yes, I like to tell stories that are true."

Then he asked, "After you have finished your true stories sometime, why don't you make up a story and the people to go with it?

"Only then will you understand what happened and why.

"It is those we live with and love and should understand who elude us."

What was Norman Maclean's story saying?

It was saying, I think, that the ones we most want to help are the ones we are often least able to help. It is a story about connecting with the people closest to us, how difficult that is to do, and how heartbreaking it is when, for whatever reason, we can't seem to do it.

If that was what the story was saying, what was it saying, if anything, to me?

I read *A River Runs Through It* at a time when I was trying to connect with someone I lived with and loved and should have understood but suddenly didn't, with someone I wanted with all my heart to help but even with all my heart, couldn't. The loss of that relationship was like a death. It filled me with grief and sadness and questions like ones the father asked his son in Norman Maclean's story.

"Are you sure you have told me everything you know about his death?" he asked.

"Everything."

"It's not much, is it?"

"No," I replied, "but you can love completely without complete understanding."

"That I have known and preached," my father said.

When I read those words, it was as if the father had preached them to me. "You can love completely without complete understanding." The words echoed in me as if off the walls of an empty cathedral in which I was the only person sitting in its pews.

It was not required of me to understand. It was required of me to love, and to go on loving, completely.

They were words I needed to hear, words I think God wanted me to hear, spoken not through the Scriptures but through a story. A story that opened up and became, for me, at least, a window of the soul.

"A great novel is a kind of conversion experience. We come away from it changed," said children's novelist Katherine Paterson.

The change may be a change in the way we look at life in general or at our own lives in particular. It may be a change in the way we think or see or feel. It may be a change in the way we look at someone on the street or someone in our own home.

It may even change the way we look at ourselves.

Not everyone, of course, feels that way about stories. Augustine's view of stories, for instance. It was similar to Plato's, who excluded poets from the ideal state because he felt their stories were at best, frivolous, and at worst, destructive in their influence. But although he sided with Plato, Augustine did confess that as a schoolboy he disliked the rote work of math and the sound of "one and one, two; two and two, four," but that he loved to hear "the burning of Troy" and "the wooden horse lined with armed men."

In junior high I took two years of Latin from a woman named Mrs. Cooper. For me, conjugating verbs—*amo, amas, amat; amamus, amatis, amant*—was like the rote work of "one and one, two; two and two, four." But once a year Mrs. Cooper broke her routine to give a book review for the school, and in the spring of my ninth-grade year the student body assembled in the auditorium to hear her review *Rascal* by Sterling North, a story about a boy and his raccoon. The story ended with the boy's realizing that his baby raccoon had grown up and that he must let it go so it could follow its natural instincts, find a mate, and start a life of its own.

> "Do as you please, my little raccoon. It's your life," I told him.
>
> He hesitated for a full minute, turned once to look back at me, then took the plunge and swam to the near shore. He had chosen to join that entrancing female somewhere in the shadows. I caught only one glimpse of them in the moonlit glade before they disappeared to begin their new life together.
>
> I left the pecans on a stump near the waterline, hoping Rascal would find them. And I paddled swiftly and desperately away from the place where we had parted.

After Mrs. Cooper's review, the book was checked out of the library for a month. When I finally got a copy, I read it and loved it all over again. Years later when I had children of my own, we got a baby raccoon and raised it until it too grew up, and until we too had to let it go.

Over the years I have read stories to my children, and one of the stories I read was *Rascal.* The story, as I was to discover years later, was not about a boy and his raccoon. It was about loving, and losing what you love. It was about growing up, about learning when to let go, and how.

Which is to say, it was about life itself.

For all of life is learning when to let go, and how. When to let go of army men. How to let go of dolls. When to let go of friends and neighborhoods and summer jobs. How to let go of childhood and adolescence. When to let go of the single life. How to let go of your children.

And someday, how to let go of life itself.

A Prayer for Revelation

Please, God,

Reveal to me through stories something of what it is like
to walk around in someone else's shoes.
Show me something about myself in the stories I read,
something that needs changing,
a thought or feeling or attitude.
Deliver me from myself, O God,
and from the parochial and sometimes prejudiced views
I have of other people, other nations,
other races, other religions.
Enlarge my heart with a story,
and change me by the characters I meet there.
May some of the light from their lives spill over into mine,
giving illumination where there was once ignorance,
interest where there was once indifference,
understanding where there was once intolerance,
compassion where there was once contempt . . .

Windows of Art

Art can warm even a chilled and sunless soul to an exalted spiritual experience. Through art we occasionally receive—indistinctly, briefly—revelations the likes of which cannot be achieved by rational thought.

It is like the small mirror of legend: you look into it but instead of yourself you glimpse for a moment the Inaccessible, a realm forever beyond reach. And your soul begins to ache...

ALEKSANDR SOLZHENITSYN
"The Nobel Lecture on Literature"

C. S. Lewis told a story of an artist who was thrown into a dungeon whose only light came from a barred window high above. In the dungeon the woman gave birth to a son. As he grew, she told him about the outside world, a world of wheat fields and mountain streams and cresting emerald waves crashing on golden shores.

But the boy couldn't understand her words. So with the drawing pad and pencils she had brought with her into the dungeon, she drew him pictures. At first she thought he understood. But one day while talking with him, she realized he didn't. He thought the outside world was made up of charcoal-gray pencil lines on faded-white backgrounds, and concluded that the world outside the dungeon was less than the world inside.

The story is a parable, showing us in much the same way the artist tried to show her son, that all we see before us are merely pencil sketches of the world beyond us. Every person is a stick-figured image of God; every place of natural beauty, a charcoal rendering of Paradise; every pleasure, a flat and faded version of the Joy that awaits us. But we need to be boosted to a window before we can see beyond the lines of our own experience. Only then will we see how big the trees are, how bright the flowers, how breathtaking the view.

"A work of art introduces us to emotions which we have never cherished before," said Abraham Heschel. "Great works produce rather than satisfy needs by giving the world fresh cravings."

When we look at a work of art, it becomes a window hewn out of the dungeon wall that separates this world from the next. And looking out that window, our soul, as Solzhenitsyn put it, "begins to ache."

Or it should, if we are looking at it the right way.

C. S. Lewis explained the right way to look at a work of art when he said: "We sit down before a picture in order to have something done to us, not that we may do things with it. The first demand any work of art makes upon us is surrender. Look. Listen. Receive."

For many of us, though, that is not what we do. We look and listen, but instead of receiving, we react; instead of surrendering, we resist; instead of coming away changed, we come away critical. And that is true whether we come away from a movie we see on Saturday night or a sermon we hear on Sunday morning.

Henri Nouwen, a Catholic priest who once taught at Notre Dame and Harvard and who now works and lives with a community of mentally handicapped people, came away deeply moved from one of Rembrandt's works of art, *The Return of the Prodigal Son*. His response to the picture was the response C. S. Lewis urged we all should have in relation to a work of art—to receive what it is offering us.

After reflecting on its impact on him, Nouwen remarked: "The painting has become a mysterious window through which I can step into the Kingdom of God."

So deep was the ache aroused in him by a mere print of the painting that Nouwen felt compelled to travel to St. Petersburg to see the original. Once there, he sat in front of that mysterious window for four hours. Looking. Listening. Receiving. In his book, *The Return of the Prodigal Son*, he recalls the experience.

> And so there I was; facing the painting that had been on my mind and in my heart for nearly three years. I was stunned by its majestic beauty. Its size, larger than life; its abundant reds, browns, and yellows; its shadowy recess and bright foreground, but most of all the light-enveloped embrace of father and son surrounded by four mysterious bystanders, all of this gripped me with an intensity far beyond my anticipation. There had been moments in which I had wondered whether the real painting might disappoint me. The opposite was true. Its grandeur and splendor made everything recede into the background and held me completely captivated.
> Rembrandt's embrace remained imprinted on my soul far more profoundly than any temporary expression of emotional support. It had brought me into touch with something within me that lies far

beyond the ups and downs of a busy life, something that represents the ongoing yearning of the human spirit, the yearning for a final return, an unambiguous sense of safety, a lasting home. While busy with many people, involved in many issues, and quite visible in many places, the homecoming of the prodigal son stayed with me and continued to take on even greater significance in my spiritual life. The yearning for a lasting home, brought to consciousness by Rembrandt's painting, grew deeper and stronger, somehow making the painter himself into a faithful companion and guide.

Having spent much more time in movie theaters than museums, I have had no encounters with art as the one Henri Nouwen had. What encounters I have had, for the most part, have been little more than captioned summaries by hurried tour guides.

Like my encounter with the art of Vincent van Gogh.

I met him at the J. Paul Getty Museum in Malibu, California, when taking my mother there, who was visiting me from out of town. What I knew about van Gogh was limited to three things. That only one of his paintings had sold in his lifetime. That at some time in his troubled life he had cut off his ear. And that he had finally ended his troubled life by committing suicide.

One other thing.

That the Getty museum had recently purchased the artist's painting, *Irises,* at auction from Sotheby's for some stratospheric figure in the tens of millions of dollars.

I first saw the painting hanging on a wall, roped off, with a guard standing next to it. My reaction to van Gogh's painting was as unlike Henri Nouwen's reaction to Rembrandt's as could possibly be imagined.

I stood, not sat, before it. And at a distance. I looked, not for four hours, not even for four minutes. A minute, maybe, that's all. My reaction? Disbelief. How could such an ordinary painting sell for so outrageous a price? Irises, of all things. A backyard, garden variety of irises. I shook my head. And I walked away.

That was the last I saw of van Gogh.

Until a few years later when I heard somewhere from someone, though I can't remember now where I heard it or from whom, that van Gogh believed in God, and at one time in his life, passionately. I recalled the song Don McLean recorded as a tribute to him. "Vincent" was the title; "Starry, starry nights," the first line. I was at a grocery store, of all places, when I heard the song again over the speakers in the ceiling. I went to the next aisle and stood under one of the speakers so I could hear the lyrics more clearly. I stood, still at a distance, but this time I listened.

Now I understand
What you tried to say to me
And how you suffered for your sanity
And how you tried to set them free.
They would not listen,
They did not know how.
Perhaps they'll listen now.

Was I one of the ones the singer was referring to, one of the ones who wouldn't listen, who didn't know how? What did the songwriter understand that I didn't? What was Vincent trying to say? And what, if anything, was he trying to say to me?

That week I went to a music store, bought the CD, and listened to "Vincent's" lyrics. I went to a bookstore, bought a three-volume collection of his letters, and started reading. I went to another bookstore, bought several books about the artist, and thumbed through the pages of his life, stopping here and there at pictures of sunflowers and birds flying over wheat fields, portraits of simple people, sad people mostly, and one of a sower in the field.

He started out in life, I discovered, wanting "to sow the words of the Bible" to poor and working-class people. In preparation for this he would sit at his desk night after night and copy page after page of the Bible, translating them into English, German, and French. "I read it daily," he wrote, "but I should like to know it by heart and to view life in the light of its words."

While in London, he went to the remotest parts of the city and preached to the poorest of the poor. He felt destined to follow in his father's vocational footsteps as a pastor, so he sought a theological education. But Vincent's temperament and zeal and eccentricities distanced him from the religious establishment. "He didn't know the meaning of submission," one of his fellow students remarked. And maybe that's why the school he attended assigned him, more as a concession than a commission, to be a "lay evangelist" in an impoverished coal-mining town.

The conditions in which the miners worked were abysmal. Laboring in the dark and gaseous bowels of the earth, they faced the dangers of poisoned air, explosions, underground flooding, and collapse of the mine itself. The long hours of backbreaking labor took their toll too. "Most of the miners," Vincent wrote, "are thin and pale from fever; they look tired and emaciated, weather-beaten and aged before their time."

On September 24, 1880, he wrote his brother Theo: "The miners and the weavers still constitute a race apart from other laborers and artisans, and I feel a great sympathy for them."

Vincent lived among the miners, sharing their poverty. He went down in the mines to be with them, breathing into his lungs the same black dust they breathed into theirs. He visited the sick among them, bandaging their wounds, praying with them. And he preached to them on Sundays, trying the best he could to infuse a little light, a little hope, a little encouragement into their coal-dark lives.

"I should be very happy if someday I could draw them," he wrote Theo, "so that those unknown or little-known types would be brought before the eyes of the people."

Before long, that is what he did.

Rilke would later write of this as the beginning of van Gogh's life as an artist. "And so he becomes what is called an evangelist, and he goes to a mining district and tells the people the story of the gospel. And while he talks, he begins to draw. And finally he doesn't even notice how he's stopped talking and is only drawing."

Because of Vincent's extreme self-denial, his fanatical zeal, and his unwillingness to follow the guidelines set before him, the governing body overseeing his ministry terminated his position. Angered and embittered, Vincent left, and, at twenty-seven years of age, embarked on what was to become his journey as an artist.

"I want you to understand clearly my conception of art," he wrote Theo at the beginning of that journey. "I want to do drawings which *touch* some people. . . . In either figure or landscape I should wish to express, not sentimental melancholy, but serious sorrow. . . . I want to progress so far that people will say of my work, he feels deeply, he feels tenderly."

Vincent was drawn to common laborers, the poor and the downtrodden, particularly. He painted pictures of a peasant woman sewing, of women working in a peat field, of farmers eating around their table after a long day of toil. He painted a young peasant with a sickle, a woman weeping, two women kneeling in prayer, a woman with a child in her lap, a girl looking at a baby in its cradle.

I tried to look at van Gogh's pictures the way Henri Nouwen looked at Rembrandt's painting. I looked. I listened. But it was like listening to a foreign language. The vocabulary of his colors, the grammar of his compositions, these were all new to me. I needed a translator, someone who could interpret this cryptic sign language.

I turned to the poet Rilke, who had spent much time studying Cezanne, Rodin, and van Gogh, among others. He had spent hour after hour in museums, studying works of art. In reading his letters, it was of some consolation to me to hear the poet admitting his eyes were also too immature on their own to see much. It was not until he had met and talked with artists themselves that he learned how to look at their work.

I turned to Vincent's letters and met him there. It was like talking with the artist himself. I listened and from him learned how to look at his pictures.

In those letters, Vincent taught me the purpose of his paintings. "In a picture, I want to say something comforting, as music is comforting. I want to paint men and women with that something of the eternal which the halo used to symbolize. . . ."

His sketch, *At Eternity's Gate*, is of a man sitting in a chair, his face buried in his hands. "In this print I have tried to express," said van Gogh, "what seems to me one of the strongest proofs of the existence . . . of God and eternity—certainly in the infinitely touching expression of such a little old man, which he himself is perhaps unconscious of, when he is sitting quietly in his corner by the fire. At the same time there is something precious, something noble, which cannot be destined for worms."

But no one seemed to understand what this impassioned artist was trying to say. It was as if it were a foreign language to them as well. Through years of rejection, loneliness, and depression, Vincent's mental state deteriorated. So did the state of his spiritual life. The erosion of faith is chronicled in the letters he wrote over the ten years that spanned his life as an artist. The Scripture quotations, references to God, and reflections of his faith, gradually grew fewer and farther between. At the same time, the anguish and despair grew greater and darker and more turbulent.

On May 8, 1889, the ailing artist was admitted to Saint-Remy asylum a few miles northeast of Arles, France. He was given a bedroom there, sparsely furnished, and a small room off it. In the meticulously researched movie about van Gogh's life, *Lust for Life*, the nun who first showed him his room at the asylum asked, "Would you like me to open the windows?"

Vincent nodded. When she opened them, he looked out on the countryside with its sun-washed fields, and it was a turning point in his life. He converted the small room off his bedroom into a studio and started once again to paint.

The window in that studio overlooked a garden. In that garden grew a plot of flowers. From that plot came his first painting at the asylum. He signed it in the lower right-hand corner, "Vincent." He titled it, simply, *Irises.* It was the painting that helped restore his sanity. And the painting, a hundred years later, before which I stood at a distance, shook my head, and walked away.

At the asylum, Vincent regained his sanity, for a time anyway. Later that year he finished the painting *Starry Night*, the one Don McLean alluded to in his song. In it we see something of the dark night of Vincent's soul. But in it we see something of the starlight too.

Of that painting, Vincent wrote: "That raises again the eternal question: Is the whole of life visible to us, or do we in fact know only the one hemisphere before we die? For my part I know nothing with any certainty, but the sight of the stars makes me dream, in the same simple way as I dream about the black dots representing towns and villages on a map."

But only Theo could see the light in Vincent's soul. Everyone else saw only the darkness, if they stopped long enough to see even that.

"There may be a great fire in our soul," wrote Vincent of his life, "yet no one ever comes to warm himself at it, and the passers-by see only a wisp of smoke coming though the chimney, and go along their way."

How sad life must have been for him. To feel so deeply, to want to communicate those feelings so passionately, and yet to have people stand off at a distance, shake their heads, and walk away. Eventually his physical, spiritual, mental, and emotional states all deteriorated. Darkness was everywhere.

In the end, only Theo understood the passion burning within Vincent, a fire that burned and burned until at last it burned out. The last spark is captured on canvas in a picture he painted in July 1890, titled simply, "Cornfield with Crows." Vincent wrote Theo about the painting. "A vast field of wheat under troubled skies," is the way he described it, "and I did not need to go out of my way to express sadness and extreme loneliness."

Somewhere in those vast fields under those troubled skies Vincent shot himself. The bullet lodged below his heart. The wound was not immediately fatal, and he was taken to his room where he was attended by a physician and where his brother rushed to his side.

At 1:30 in the morning, on July 29, 1890, while Theo was holding Vincent in his arms, the artist spoke his last words.

"*La tristesse durea.*"

"The sadness will never go away."

Someone once said that you are a success if, at the end of your life, the people who knew you best are the ones who respect you most. The two people that knew Vincent best were his brother and his mother. "He has a great heart that is always searching for something to do for others," his brother wrote of him. Not a bad epitaph. I would settle for it in a heartbeat. "Vincent's letters," wrote his mother, "which contain so many interesting things, prove that with all his peculiarities, he yet shows a warm interest in the poor; that surely will not remain unobserved by God."

It saddened me, shamed me even, that his life had been unobserved by me, and his work, by me, so casually dismissed. But his life, I'm certain, as his mother was certain, did not go unobserved by God. Nor were his works casually dismissed. Not by God, anyway.

Through his pictures and his letters, through a movie and a song about him, I saw the artist and something of the artist's soul. But I saw something else. I saw through him something of the great artist of souls—Jesus. "Christ," said van Gogh, "is more of an artist than the artists; he works in the living spirit and the living flesh; he makes *men* instead of statues."

Like Vincent, Jesus drew our attention to a sower in the field, birds of the air, flowers of the field, faces of the poor. Like Vincent, he has, to borrow Don McLean's words, "eyes that know the darkness in my soul," and hands, like an artist's that soothed "weathered faces lined in pain." Like Vincent, he put frames around "ragged men in ragged clothes." And like Vincent, he "tried to set them free."

But unlike Vincent, who died from a self-inflicted wound, Jesus died from wounds inflicted by others. Unlike Vincent, whose last days were filled with despair, on the night in which Jesus was betrayed, He encouraged His disciples not to let their hearts be troubled for He was going to prepare a place for them in His Father's house. Even in the pain of His own cross, He encouraged a thief on the cross next to Him with the hope of heaven. And even in His forsakenness, Jesus entrusted His spirit to His Father's hands.

In spite of some similarities, much separates the two artists, both in the way they lived and the way they died. But maybe it is not too much to suggest that even in their deaths they had something in common.

"A man of sorrows, acquainted with grief."

"The sadness will never go away."

There is something of Vincent's sadness and Christ's sorrow mingled in the last lines of Don McLean's song. Can you hear it?

Now I think I know
What you tried to say to me
And how you suffered for your sanity
And how you tried to set them free.
They would not listen,
They're not listening still,
Perhaps they never will.

Passersby stood at a distance and criticized both artists. They shook their heads at their pictures. And they walked away.

What were these two artists trying to say, and what were they trying to say to me and to you?

"Look at the pictures" is what I think they were saying. And if you look with the right eyes, those pictures will become windows leading out of the dungeon so the prodigal part of us can find its way home.

A Prayer for Humility

Help me, O God,

To have the humility to sit at the feet of great art,
whether it is a painting or a person on the street,
a scene from a movie or a score from a musical,
a sunset or a psalm,
and to look and to listen and to receive
what is being offered me there.
Give me the grace to submit to its scrutiny,
seeking not to do something to it,
but that it might do something to me;
seeking not in some way to judge it,
but that it might in some way judge me . . .

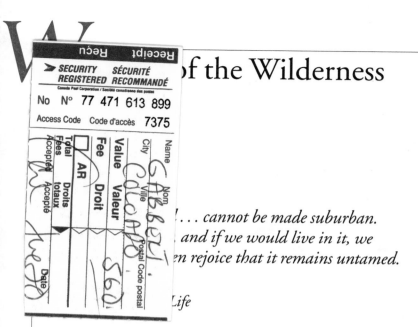

... cannot be made suburban.
and if we would live in it, we
en rejoice that it remains untamed.

Life

*OLD TESTAMENT TYPOLOGY IN
MATTHEW'S AND LUKE'S TEMPTATION NARRATIVES*

———————

*A Thesis
Presented to
the Faculty of the Department of Semitic Languages
and Old Testament Exegesis
Dallas Theological Seminary*

———————

*In Partial Fulfillment
of the Requirements for the Degree
Master of Theology*

———————

*by
Kenneth Paxton Gire, II
April 4, 1978*

That was the first page of my master's thesis, which was also the last page of my four years of theological education. It has the proper form, proper margins, and a proper "Introduction," which reads:

> The purpose of this thesis is to exegetically establish a typological correspondence between Israel and her wilderness testings and Christ and His wilderness testings and between Adam and Christ. The temptation narratives of Matthew and Luke will be used as a focus of exegesis. The goal is twofold: first, to explicate a theory of typology; second, to exegete the temptation narratives to uncover the author's intention. It will be demonstrated that a studied attempt is made to compare and contrast Christ with Israel in Matthew and Christ with Adam in Luke.

It sounds like I know what I'm talking about, doesn't it? And with the first page full of single-spaced footnotes, it looks like I know what I'm talking about. Certainly after four years of theological education, I should know what I'm talking about.

There was only one problem.

As of April 4, 1978, I had never been through a wilderness that even remotely resembled the one about which I had written with such authority. Yet a month later, in the ceremonious turn of a tassel, I became a "Master of Theology."

At other graduation ceremonies I have attended over the years, I have heard, as I'm sure you have heard, someone at sometime or another extol the poem "Invictus," by W. E. Henley.

It matters not how strait the gate,
How charged with punishments the scroll,
I am the master of my fate:
I am the captain of my soul.

Being the captain of our soul, like going off to sea, has always been something of a romantic theme in literature. And, as we send off graduates from the safe harbors of higher education to the high seas of whatever vocational course they have charted for their lives, Henley's poem, as we wave from the dock, seems the most appropriate thing to say.

Until their ship hits a reef.

Then what do we say?

Every man for himself? Cling for dear life to whatever's left floating? Hope for dear life that some other captain will come to your rescue? Dog-paddle for shore?

A captain whose ship is dashed against the rocks is no more the master of his fate than I was a master of theology. But it took my life running aground before I realized that. When it did, I found myself washed up on a lonely stretch of shore where the only way back to civilization was by land, land that led through an uncertain and unsafe wilderness.

When I graduated from seminary, I pushed off from the dock, having charted a course to teach in a secular university and write during the summers, though I had no formal education in writing and didn't know what I would write about. The course quickly and unexpectedly changed. As I was being turned down by every institution of higher learning to which I applied, I helped start that small rural church that I mentioned earlier.

After two years there, I felt a gentle wind filling my sails, and something in the wind—Was it the Spirit of God?—telling me it was time to start writing. That's when I attempted my first book, a short children's novel about a year in the lives of a set of twins, a boy and a girl, one of whom was mentally handicapped.

Writing the book was an exhilarating experience, and when I finished, I began rearranging deck chairs to accommodate this sprawling passion that had boarded my life. I left the church and took a job selling oil-field equipment, hoping to earn enough money so I could take off some time to continue writing. After two-and-a-half years selling pumping units and sucker rods, I was able to do that. It was a dream come true. I moved our family to east Texas to the town of Nacogdoches, where every day I walked to the college library and wrote from eight to five.

My ship had come in.

What I didn't know was that it had come in on its way to running aground. As its hull scraped the shoals, I discovered that the writing life was not the romantic cruise the travel brochures made it out to be but rather, one jarring rejection after another.

It was a painfully introspective time for me, trying to get a grip on my elusive craft, trying to find out who I was, which proved equally elusive, and trying to support a wife and four kids on the words I put on 8 ½" x 11" sheets of paper.

For two years nothing sold. Two years of going to work every day and never coming home with a paycheck. Someone once said that writing is the only profession in which one can make no money without looking ridiculous. But at the end of two years, if I wasn't looking that way, I was certainly feeling that way.

When our savings ran out, we liquidated our IRA, sold a car and some furniture. When that money ran out, we put our house up for sale. It seemed like the appropriate, however improvident, next step. Was it? Was it walking by faith or just wishing upon a star? Was I being steadfast or just stubborn? I couldn't tell. I was determined to write and to make a living at it. Was I too determined? Or not determined enough? I didn't know.

It was a recessionary time in Texas when we tried to sell our house, and houses weren't selling. I hung wallpaper to make ends meet. So many times I would come home from work with sore knees and a sunken heart, feeling so foolish for squandering our security on pipe dreams and return postage for publishers.

I kept a journal of those times, my thoughts clinging to some passages from the Bible, a few stanzas of poetry, an occasional scene from a movie, anything. But going into my third year of clinging, I was tired and starting to lose my grip.

Jan. 22, 1985, Nacogdoches

It is so discouraging being on the outside. With no job and no material security and everyone else seeming so ordered and established. Adrift. Cut loose from any moorings & far from harbor. It is a dizzy and sick feeling. A lonely feeling. I hate it.

Feb. 20, 1985, Nacogdoches

I have come to a point of emotional and spiritual exhaustion. Drained dry, a drop of life at a time. I can no longer read my Bible, feeling forsaken. I can no longer pray, feeling ignored. It is a great hurt. If God is truly a great God, he can love me even though I can no longer look into His face or call out to Him in prayer. If He cannot, then my prayers and devotions are ill-spent anyway, and my time is better used elsewhere.

Nov. 26, 1985, Nacogdoches

I don't know who is wrestling against me, God or Satan, but whoever it is, I surrender. . . . I have done everything in my power to serve

Him in the way I feel most qualified and effective. I have depleted all my material resources, my prayers, my energies, my heart. I don't know what else I can do. I've given all I can give. And now I give up. . . . He has stripped me of all my self-worth, my self-respect, and now I stand naked, impotent, and ashamed before Him. . . . Today, someone has won a victory. I don't know if it is God or Satan—but I know who lost—me.

During those last days in Nacogdoches, as I was trying to figure out what God wanted from me, I came across a passage of Scripture that I noted in my journal.

April 9, 1985, Nacogdoches
Though the fig tree does not bud
    and there are no grapes on the vines,
though the olive crop fails
    and the fields produce no food,
though there are no sheep in the pen
    and no cattle in the stalls,
yet I will rejoice in the LORD,
    I will be joyful in God my Savior.
The Sovereign LORD is my strength;
    he makes my feet like the feet of a deer,
    he enables me to go on the heights.
Habakkuk 3:17–19

I couldn't rejoice during those days. My faith wasn't that strong. But I could believe, from the budding azaleas and hydrangeas emerging from the east Texas winter, that there was at least the hope of something emerging from my life as well. As I look back on it, that passage was a window of the soul, revealing what God wanted from me. He wanted me to trust that spring would follow winter. To live by faith, not by sight. And to have Him, not success, be the source of my joy.

Six months later the house finally sold, and my wife's parents let us move in a vacant farmhouse they owned in Poolville, Texas. For the next year we lived off the equity of the house we had sold. I continued to write. And I continued to tell myself that spring would come. But it didn't. It was so humiliating to face friends and relatives and have to answer well-meaning questions like, "How's the writing going?"—all the while knowing it wasn't going anywhere, but having trouble admitting that to myself, let alone, to anybody else.

To protect myself from the embarrassment of those encounters, I withdrew. To Poolville. There I was—there we all were, all six of us—in the middle of nowhere. With no savings, no retirement fund, no home of our own, no job, no medical insurance—and no future. Or so it seemed. There were snakes outside the house, scorpions inside, and the scorn of the Texas sun glaring down on us. Or was it the scorn of God? I didn't know.

I couldn't understand, when I felt so passionately about writing, worked so diligently, sacrificed so completely, why nothing was working out. Where was God in all this? Why wasn't He helping me? I needed His help, wanted His help, asked for His help. Didn't He hear the words I prayed, see the tears I cried, understand the confusion I felt? Didn't He care?

In Ernest Hemingway's book *The Old Man and the Sea*, he expressed something of what I felt when he described what it was like for a fish on the other end of a fishing line. "The punishment of the hook is nothing. The punishment of hunger, and that he is against something that he does not comprehend, is everything."

Suddenly I found myself against a God who baited me and then set the hook. But it was not the punishment of the hook. That was nothing. It was the hunger in my soul, and that I was against something, or something was against me, that I did not comprehend. That was everything.

As physical hunger intensifies with the absence of food, so spiritual hunger intensifies with the absence of God. That is why the wilderness plays such an important role in our lives, as it did in the lives of Moses, David, Elijah, Job. The wilderness is where we experience prolonged periods of God's absence. For me, that was Poolville. For you, it may be Los Angeles or Odessa, General

Motors or graduate school. For me, it was a crisis brought on by a change of careers. For you, it may be a crisis brought on by cancer or divorce or some other struggle.

Whatever the wilderness, wherever the wilderness, it is in that wilderness where we learn that we do not live by bread alone but by every word that proceeds from the mouth of God, that His word is not only the most natural food for our soul but the most necessary.

I will never forget how hungry I was for some word from Him to let me know that He saw me stranded there in Poolville, that He heard my prayers, and, most of all, that He cared. I will never forget, too, how He fed me. Through a small window in our front door, something like manna was offered me, I believe, by the hand of God.

I jotted down the experience in my journal.

Jan. 6, 1986, Poolville

A family of stray cats (a mother & three kittens) has sought refuge from the cold underneath the pier-and-beam foundation of our house. They are timid & fearful, scared of coming too close to us in spite of our gentle efforts at coaxing them. Every night I leave some food out with some milk. As I peek through the blinds of the front porch door, I see them cautiously approach their daily allotment, ears erect, eyes darting. They are cold and scared and, I suppose, the world has shown them little kindness—if not outright cruelty.

As I bend the blind, looking down on them as they eat, I feel a certain kindred spirit with them—the cold, the scared, the abandoned— and I hope that somewhere God is bending a blind to look down on me.

Every night I watched as one by one, a tentative step at a time, the gray-and-white kittens came out. I tried to lure them into the house by opening the door and leaving a trail of food for them to follow, hoping they would come just far enough in so I could close the door and catch one. But they were too wary for that.

So one day at dusk I put a big cardboard box in front of the crawl space opening with some cat food at the end of it. I waited. And waited. And finally . . . the sound of a tentative paw. Then another. Step by scratchy step. Until the kitten reached the end of the box. And then I flipped it over.

Gotcha!

I brought the box inside. We all gathered around the square rim of cardboard, nosing down for a good look. I put on a pair of leather work gloves and picked up the ball of brindled fluff. The kitten didn't move. Not a muscle. Not a whisker. It was as lifeless as a stuffed animal.

After we oohed and aahed over it a while, I put it in the bathroom with a saucer of milk and some food and closed the door so it could get used to the foreign surroundings. An hour or so later I came back. As soon as I opened the door, the kitten shot to a corner of the tiled bathroom and wedged itself there. It arched its back and hissed, taking a swipe at me with its paw when I approached. With my gloved hand, I reached for it. It slashed at the glove and bit into the leather, making all sorts of fierce little sounds, spitting, hissing, its eyes wild with anger.

What the kitten didn't know was that all I wanted to do was to draw it close, to give it a safe and warm place in our house, feed it so it didn't have to hunt down its food. I wanted to take care of it, give it a better life, pet it, and look after it. That's all. I didn't want to hurt it. But how would a kitten born in the wild know that?

Suddenly I realized.

I was that kitten. Scared stiff one minute; spitting mad the next. Was that what God was wanting to do with me? Draw me close? Give me shelter, food, look after me? But the shelter I was wanting was the security of a job, not the security of His arms. The food I was wanting was from the grocery store, not from His hand. And I could look after myself—thank you very much—I just needed a break, that was all.

The God who now held me in the clutches of His hand was so foreign to the God I had once held in mine. Was it His face I was scratching at, His hand I was biting?

That image of the scared kitten stayed with me, and softened me. I didn't want to scratch and bite anymore. I was through fighting. But not crying. Every day as the sun set in the expansive Texas sky, I cried out to God to give me my life back, to rescue me from the wilderness. He taught me that the way out of the wilderness was on a road paved with tears.

The road led to southern California—and a job. Of all the jobs I had applied for, it was the only one that said yes. And it was a writing job. I couldn't believe it. Someone was actually paying me to do what I loved.

The fig tree had budded.

Spring had come.

Finally.

When I first listened to the call of God to write, little did I realize it was a call to the wilderness. But it was there, not seminary, that God prepared me to be a writer. The wilderness was a place of pain, of humiliation, of uncertainty, of loneliness and desperation. All of which were necessary for me to experience if I was to be the writer I needed to be, wanted to be, prayed to be. How could I know the feelings of the desperate if I had not been desperate myself? How could I know the feelings of the poor if I had not been poor myself? How could I know the feelings of the confused if I had not been confused myself? Or depressed myself? Or abandoned?

Seminary prepared me to use my gift. The wilderness prepared me to live my life. And it will prepare you to live yours. But your wilderness will be different from mine. And the windows you will be shown will be different from the ones shown to me. The education of the wilderness is not standardized, like seminary. It is individualized, for you and you alone as it was for me and me alone. For each and every one who enters the wilderness, what is shown them is for their eyes and their eyes only. For their ears. And for their heart.

Something about that is like being on the frontier with all its risks and uncertainties. And that's a little unsettling.

"We don't like risk," said Howard Macy, "and even though the frontiers of spiritual growth require it, we prefer to avoid it. Not only would we like to have the frontiers of the spirit scouted out for us, we would also like to have the frontier fully tamed and settled, like a new suburban development with well-lighted streets and sewers installed, established zoning codes, houses built and finished save for seeding the lawn and planting the shrubs, shopping centers nearby, and adequate police protection. No pioneering for us—no danger from the dark wild, no felling trees or clearing boulders so that we can plant a subsistence garden, no climbing mountain passes or fording swollen streams. We prefer comfortable safety to risk."

Seminary was the suburbs of my spiritual life.

It was a safe neighborhood where I could learn about God and the Bible and the spiritual life. I could choose my own well-lighted course of study, and, within the established limits of evangelical zoning codes, I could landscape at least a portion of my curriculum. I could choose morning classes or ones in the afternoon. Choose to have summers off or take summer school and lighten my load in the fall. I could even choose the topic for my thesis.

All of this, and, if I paid the tuition, showed up for classes, did the required work, I would become in four years a master of theology.

It was all so safe.

And safe is what we all really want to be, isn't it? It was what the children wanted to be in C. S. Lewis's *The Lion, the Witch and the Wardrobe*, when they first heard that the true king of Narnia was a lion.

Susan asks the Beavers. "Is he—quite safe? I shall feel rather nervous about meeting a lion."

"That you will, dearie, and no mistake," said Mrs. Beaver, "if there's anyone who can appear before Aslan without their knees knocking, they're either braver than most or else just silly."

"Then he isn't safe?" said Lucy.

"Safe?" said Mr. Beaver. "Don't you hear what Mrs. Beaver tells you? Who said anything about safe? 'Course he isn't safe. But he's good."

The wilderness taught me theology and how incapable I was of ever becoming its master. There was nothing safe or systematic about it. No syllabus, no class notes, no textbook. At the beginning, I didn't know how long the course would last or what tuition I would have to pay before it was over. I disagreed with my teacher, sometimes angrily, sometimes disrespectfully. I complained about the course load and wanted to drop the class. But it was a required course, I was to discover, not an elective, and this was the only time it was being offered. I raised my hand, waved my hand, persistently, but my questions were not acknowledged, let alone, answered. At least, not in my time or on my terms.

The wilderness was my thesis. It was where I had to prove to myself who God really is. It was all original research. No quotes from secondary sources. I had to write it a painful word at a time, a puzzling paragraph at a time, page after page, until my thesis was proved. There was no proper form to follow. All the margins were off; the spacing, erratic; the pages, out of sequence. It was a mess.

But it was *my* mess.

And out of it came the message of my life, or at least, the beginnings of it. And now I am able to know from my own life—not somebody else's—who God really is.

As the emerging nation of Israel left the wilderness, where they had wandered for the past forty years, and crossed the Jordan River into the Promised Land, they were shown a window revealing the purpose for those disorienting years. That window is preserved for our viewing in Deuteronomy 8. The first thing they were shown was that it was God who had led them into the wilderness. It wasn't Moses or Aaron or simply their own inept sense of direction. It was also important for them to see *why* He had led them there—"to humble them, to test them, and to do good to them in the end." (v. 16)

To do good to them in the end.

"'Course he isn't safe," was the conclusion I reached in the wilderness. "But he's good."

A *Prayer for Transformation*

Help me, O God,

To realize the role the wilderness plays
in my continuing education.
Thank You that even in the wilderness there are windows,
revealing what You want from me,
showing that You care,
and clarifying, when I look back,
what You were doing in my life.
Thank You, God, for the wild and untamed theology
You have taught me in the wilderness,
and for the assurance that,
though You are not safe,
you are good . . .

Windows of Poetry

... For in him we live and move and have our being. As some of your own poets have said, "We are his offspring."

THE APOSTLE PAUL
From his address to the Athenians
Acts 17:28

The waters of truth that run through this world sometimes flow through the most surprising channels. God spoke to Job through a whirlwind, of all places. He spoke to Elijah too, but not through the whirlwind. The whirlwind passed him by without a word, which came instead through the gentle rustling left in its wake.

God spoke to David through Shimei, of all people, a man who taunted him with curses, pelted him with rocks, and showered him with dirt. Could the word of God flow through such turbid waters? David seemed to think so. Then there's Balaam's donkey. How do we explain that? And Pilate's wife, a pagan, and yet the dream she had about Christ the night before his crucifixion was true.

If we accept the premise that all truth is God's truth, then however winding its tributaries or turbulent its waters, if we follow its currents far enough upstream, it will lead to God. Sometimes a trickle of that truth even finds its way into a poem.

Poems are not places we generally expect to hear God's voice, but it is where the apostle Paul heard it. In his address to the Athenians he cites the works of the Greek poets Epimenides, Cleanthes, and Aratus, not only agreeing with them—"As some of your own poets have said, 'We are his offspring'"—but using their texts as the basis of his argument against idolatry. "Therefore," Paul concludes, "since we are God's offspring, we should not think that the divine being is like gold or silver or stone—an image made by man's design and skill."

There are no persons so pagan that God cannot speak through them. There is no place so remote that God's voice cannot be heard there. At any time, in any place, through any means, God can speak to us. Sometimes He speaks through a wild wind raging through our lives; other times, through the calm rhythms rippling through a poem.

A few months after I had settled into my new job, I came across such a poem. Some of what you see in that poem may seem obscure, as some of it seemed to me then and seems to me still. But some of what you see may, as it did for me, forever change the way you look at life.

Sept. 1, 1986, Fullerton

"The Man Watching" by Rainer Maria Rilke.

*I can tell by the way the trees beat, after
so many dull days, on my worried windowpanes
that a storm is coming,
and I hear the far-off fields say things
I can't bear without a friend,
I can't love without a sister.*

*The storm, the shifter of shapes, drives on
across the woods and across time,
and the world looks as if it had no age:
the landscape, like a line in the psalm book,
is seriousness and weight and eternity.*

*What we choose to fight is so tiny!
What fights with us is so great!
If only we would let ourselves be dominated
as things do by some immense storm,
we would become strong too, and not need names.*

*When we win, it's with small things,
and the triumph itself makes us small.
What is extraordinary and eternal
does not want to be bent by us.
I mean the Angel who appeared
to the wrestlers of the Old Testament:
when the wrestlers' sinews
grew long like metal strings,
he felt them under his fingers
like chords of deep music.*

*Whoever was beaten by this Angel
(who often simply declined the fight)
went away proud and strengthened
and great from that harsh hand,
that kneaded him as if to change his shape.
Winning does not tempt that man.*

This is how he grows: by being defeated, decisively,
by constantly greater beings.

I sensed when I first read the poem that it was showing me something about myself. But what?

"It is not wisdom, but foolishness, that is stubborn," said Sophocles. "Look at the trees. By embracing the movements of the tempest they preserve their tender branches; but if they rear against the wind they are carried off, roots and all."

Had I been simply struggling with getting a career started, as all people struggle when they're starting out, or had some immense storm galed against me when I was in the wilderness? Had I embraced the movements of the tempest, or just stubbornly reared against the wind?

Had I been Jacob, longing for God's blessing, but in my own time, on my own terms, trying to pry it from His hand?

Is this how I was to grow—as a person, as a writer—by being defeated, decisively, by constantly greater beings? Not by mastering theology but by being thrown to the ground and held there, face mashed against the dirt, breath knocked out of me, gasping for air, ligaments straining at the joints, burning, popping, tearing loose.

According to the biblical story, Jacob, after wrestling till dawn, finally did walk away with God's blessing.

But he walked with a limp.

And he walked that way the rest of his life.

Would I?

In Poolville I learned the hard lessons of the wilderness. When I finished my final semester there, I was not walking across the stage in a cap and gown. I was limping away, sweaty and dirty. I wasn't being handed a diploma but rather a crippling defeat.

My study of God in seminary was systematic; my experience of Him was not. He came on me like a sudden and terrifying storm, like a wrestler jumping me from behind and overpowering me. In the fury of the storm I was given a choice: Bend or be broken. In the grip of the wrestler I was forced to decide to: surrender and go away limping, or keep struggling and maybe never get up to go anywhere at all.

The images in Rilke's poem dawned in my consciousness to burn away the morning haze left from that disorienting night. I could see now that it was God who had wrestled with me in that wilderness, throwing me to the ground and dislocating my hip. And now, with the haze gone, I could see something else.

In dislocating my hip, God had taught me to cling.

In making me limp, He had taught me to lean . . .

not on my own two legs, but on Him.

Before entering the wilderness, I came across Tennyson's poem *Idylls of the King* and found it pooling with truth. The word *idyll* means "little picture," and the poem is a series of them, chronicling the reign of King Arthur at the dawn of English civilization. The poem ends with a section titled "The Passing of Arthur" in which the dying king is placed on a funeral barge by Bedivere, one of Arthur's knights. As Bedivere pushes the barge out to sea, he bids Arthur a final farewell, and the king responds with a few last words of his own.

> *And slowly answer'd Arthur from the barge:*
> *"The old order changeth, yielding place to new,*
> *And God fulfils himself in many ways,*
> *Lest one good custom should corrupt the world.*
> *Comfort thyself: What comfort is in me?*
> *I have lived my life, and that which I have done*
> *May He within himself make pure! but thou,*
> *If thou shouldst never see my face again,*
> *Pray for my soul. More things are wrought by prayer*
> *Than this world dreams of. Wherefore, let thy voice*
> *Rise like a fountain for me night and day.*
> *For what are men better than sheep or goats*
> *That nourish a blind life within the brain,*

If, knowing God, they lift not hands of prayer
Both for themselves and those who call them friend?
For so the whole round earth is every way
Bound by gold chains about the feet of God.

That portion of the poem was like an oasis for me during my time in the wilderness. It was a little pool of truth that somehow gave me the strength to keep praying.

I wasn't sure how I had gotten into the wilderness I was in, and I didn't know how to get out. Every day at dusk I stood in the corner of the yard, leaning on the fence to watch another day die. And every day as the sun was interred on the horizon, bequeathing its colors to the clouds, I prayed for a way out of the wilderness.

What I learned in that corner of the yard was that prayer *is* the way out.

How many more things have I found my way out of because of prayer? Or found my way into? Certainly somebody's prayers helped me, when I was a teenager, find my way into Young Life.

Many people know that Young Life is a ministry to high school students. Some know that is was started by a young seminary student named Jim Rayburn. But few know that he started the ministry at Gainesville High School. Fewer still know why. Why Gainesville? It was sixty miles from where he was attending seminary. Why not Highland Park or some other Dallas school?

Listening to Rayburn's explanation, we learn why. "Across the street from the high school a group of elderly women had been meeting for six years, every Monday morning, getting down on their knees in the living room of dear old Mrs. Frazier's. They prayed every Monday morning for six years, long before I ever heard of Gainesville, Texas, for the high-school kids across the street. I was there a year before I heard of that prayer meeting. I used to go over there with those five or six old ladies and get down on my knees with them after that club started to roll. That was the thing the Lord used to start it."

Jim Rayburn went to Gainesville because six elderly women prayed. But the women prayed only for the kids at Gainesville High. Who, looking in on those elderly women on their knees, would have ever thought that their clasped hands would be the hands that midwifed the Young Life Campaign, a world wide organization that has touched the lives of countless teenagers? Though the ministry was birthed in 1939, no one would argue that it was conceived six years earlier.

Prayer. "That was the thing the Lord used to start it."

That is the thing He uses still.

"Pray without ceasing," Paul tells us.

Tennyson tells us why. "More things are wrought by prayer than this world dreams of. . . . for so the whole round earth is every way bound by gold chains about the feet of God."

Who knows how many people prayed to pull me out of the wilderness? I knew of a few, and to those few I enclosed a copy of Tennyson's poem in a Christmas card. Who knows what all was wrought by their prayers? More than this world dreams of, I'm sure.

I understood, even in the wilderness, that God is sovereign. But He is a sovereign in chains. I didn't understand that until I read Tennyson. God has ordained His kingdom to come, but He has ordained it to come on the links of our prayers.

Maybe that is how every good thing from heaven comes.

A chain of events forged from the seemingly inconsequential links of our prayers.

A collective pull.

Then His will is done on earth as it is in heaven,
and in Poolville as it was in Gainesville.

A *Prayer for Understanding*

Help me, God,

To realize it is in being crippled that I learn to cling, and in limping that I learn to lean,
that victory comes not in how courageously I struggle
but in how completely I surrender,
and that this is how I am to grow,
by being defeated,
decisively,
by constantly greater things.
Help me to understand that Your power is perfected in weakness,
so that when I am rendered weak,
You are given the opportunity to be shown strong.
Help me to understand, too,
that "more things are wrought by prayer than this world dreams of,
for so the whole round earth is every way
bound in gold chains about the feet of God . . ."

Windows of Movies

Far more than any other influence, more than school, more even than home—my attitudes, dreams, preconceptions and pre-conditions for life had been irreversibly shaped five and a half thousand miles away in a place called Hollywood.

DAVID PUTTNAM
Producer of Chariots of Fire

The movies you choose to see can be a window into your personality," said Stuart Fischoff, professor of media psychology at Cal State Los Angeles. They can also be a window through which God speaks.

There have been times in my life, as I'm sure there have been in yours, when I've been watching a movie in a theater and a scene is so poignant, a line of dialogue so piercing, or a strain of music so stirring, that it sweeps me away as suddenly and as turbulently as the tornado swept Dorothy away in *The Wizard of Oz*. For a moment, and sometimes for only the briefest of moments, I am taken out of my black-and-white world and plopped down in a world rich with emotional color. And sometimes at those moments I sense something being offered to the innermost part of me.

One of those moments came while I was watching the movie *An Officer and a Gentleman*. The story is about a self-serving recruit, played by Richard Gere, who enters the Naval Aviation Officer Candidate School so he can get his "wings" and fly jets. But before he can graduate to flight school, he must survive a grueling thirteen weeks of mental and physical conditioning. And he must survive the drill sergeant, played by Lou Gossett, who is determined to break him in or boot him out. While the other recruits are given leave for the weekend, Gere is forced to stay on that base, where he is run through a torturous obstacle course. The drill sergeant rides him hard, getting in his face, yelling at him, taunting him, trying to get him to quit. But Gere takes it all and doesn't quit.

Finally, while the persevering recruit is doing sit-ups in the rain, the drill sergeant tells him he's finished, through, discharged from the service. And it breaks him. Through his tears, Gere pleads: "You can't do it to me. I got nowhere else to go. . . . I got nowhere else to go."

That moment in the movie had a profound impact on me. When I was going through my own grueling experiences in the wilderness and being forced to give up what I loved doing most, that scene came back to me in a powerful way. I knew what Richard Gere's character felt. I knew the determination he had to get his wings and the fear he had of not getting them. I knew the rigors of the obstacle course and the agony of endless repetitions of meaningless exercises. I knew because I was the new recruit doing sit-ups in the rain before a stern and unrelenting drill sergeant. "You can't do it to me," I remember crying out to God. "I got nowhere else to go. . . . I got nowhere else to go."

Where was I to go if things didn't work out with my writing? Back to youth work, pastoring, selling oil-field equipment, hanging wallpaper? For some reason I wasn't allowed to go where my heart was, and now I was being discharged, sent back to where it wasn't. And how could I do that without something in me dying?

"I got nowhere else to go" became my prayer. "I got nowhere else to go."

That moment in the movie reinforced Rilke's images of the storm and tree and of Jacob and the angel and images I had seen of the kitten I had caught. Like separate but interconnected pieces of a puzzle, the images came together to form a composite. That picture was a window into who I was, what God was doing in my life, and why. Despite all appearances, He was not wanting to make me quit; He was wanting to prepare me for my commission. The wilderness was just the boot camp I had to go through before I could get my wings.

Movies take the common crystal of human experience, cut it, polish it, and hold it up to the light of a 35mm projector so those sitting in the dark can see it sparkle, and, leaving the theater, take something of that sparkle with them. Of course, not all movies are made with such noble ends in mind. And of the ones that are, not all sparkle, for movies reflect the interior landscape of the soul, with all its peaks and valleys, its farmlands and wastelands, its haunting canyons and hopeful horizons.

For all the negatives that can be said about the movies, what can be said that is positive of almost all movies is that they reflect, at a very fundamental level, the longings of the soul: the longing that good triumph over evil, that truth wins out, that the drama of life brings out the hero in us, that a good character in the course of the drama grows better, wiser, more understanding, and that a bad character, if not redeemed, is at least brought to justice, and that in the end there is a happy ending, which is none other than a dim reflection, I think, of our longing for heaven.

It is without question an incredibly powerful art form, and it is that because it speaks to those longings. It doesn't always speak politely or eloquently or even accurately, but it does speak to the deepest places of the soul.

Art, music, and literature all come together in a movie, and when they all come together just right, something beautiful happens. A window opens, and you glimpse something in yourself that has been hidden from you for maybe all of your life. Or you glimpse something in someone else. Or, in a rare moment of transcendence, you glimpse something beyond.

In an interview with *The Door*, Garrison Keillor said, "If you can't go to church and, for at least a moment, be given transcendence; if you can't go to church and pass briefly from this life into the next; then I can't see why anyone should go. Just a brief moment of transcendence causes you to come out of church a changed person."

I have experienced what Garrison Keillor described more in movie theaters than I have in churches. Why? I can't say for sure. Maybe it's the generation I grew up in that I can't quite get away from. Maybe the movies appeal more to the artistic side of me in ways that well-crafted, three-point sermons don't. I don't know.

But movies don't always tell the truth, don't always enlighten, don't always inspire. What they do on a fairly consistent basis is give you an experience of transcendence. They let you lose yourself in somebody else's story. And sometimes in losing yourself you find yourself, or at least, a part of yourself. It may be a part of yourself you didn't even know needed finding. It may be a wounded part or a callused part that you find. It may be a very beautiful part or a very ugly part. A part that needed to grow up or maybe a part that needed to go back and become a child again. A part that needed to understand, maybe, or to forgive. Or maybe it was a part that needed to die, or maybe one that instead needed to be born.

Movies give you the opportunity for a couple of hours to look at somebody else's life. And sometimes that can change you.

In his "Nobel Lecture on Literature," Aleksandr Solzhenitsyn said that art and literature "both hold the key to a miracle: to overcome man's ruinous habit of learning only from his own experience, so that the experience of others passes him by without profit. Making up for man's scant time on earth, art transmits between men the entire accumulated load of another being's life experiences with all its hardships, colors, and juices. It recreates—lifelike—the experience of other men, so that we can assimilate it as our own."

Schindler's List was that kind of art. It allowed us to witness the tragic experiences of others who lived across the globe from us, spoke a different language from us, practiced different customs from us, different beliefs. It allowed us a look into their lives, a look that the passage of time has rendered inaccessible, except through testimonies and memories and works of art like this movie.

Schindler's List was, I believe, a way of not only bringing something of the past back to life but bringing something of that past to justice. Showing the horrors of the Holocaust to a broad audience brought the guilty into the courtroom of the human heart. It kept us from looking away. It involved us deeply and emotionally. It called on our conscience to pronounce a verdict, and called us to a commitment to make sure this tragedy never happens again.

The movie holds the key to a miracle, if only we would take the key that is offered us into our hands and into our hearts.

Hoop Dreams is another such film. How many people from the secure streets of suburbia would drive through the uncertain streets of the inner city, let alone stop for a look around, let alone visit for several years to try to understand the lives of the people who lived there?

And yet this is what the filmmakers did. They followed two inner-city youths from junior high to college as they pursued their dream of becoming professional basketball players. The filmmakers take us not only into their neighborhoods but into their homes, into their living rooms and dining rooms. Into the locker rooms of their dreams. Into the back alleys of their despair. We see the struggle of young boys trying to grow up and get out of the ghetto. We see the struggle of mothers trying to make ends meet, to keep the family together, make a life for themselves and their children. We see the drugs and the graffiti and the crime, but we also see religious roots struggling to take hold in the cracks of the inner-city sidewalks. Something we would never see if we were just passing through the neighborhood.

Other movies hold other keys. *The Elephant Man* is one that does. In my opinion it is one of the top five movies ever made. It is the true story of a man with a rare disease that led to his grotesque appearance and how people treated him based on that appearance. The film helps you see that it was not the Elephant Man who was grotesque but the people who treated him with such cruelty. Had I seen the film earlier in my life, maybe I would have drawn the courage from it to stand up for a mentally handicapped kid who went to my junior high and who was the brunt of so many people's practical jokes. Maybe it would have helped me find the words to say something, do something. Maybe it would have given me the eyes to see beyond the handicap and discover the boy's heart, which must have broken every day of the school year.

Another movie that holds a key of understanding is *Shadowlands*. It is the story of C. S. Lewis and the loss of his wife to cancer. At the end of the movie, Lewis makes a profound comment. "Why love if losing hurts so much? I have no answers, only the life I have lived. Twice in that life I was given the choice, as a boy and as a man. The boy chose safety. The man chose suffering. The pain now is part of the happiness then. That's the deal."

The truth of those words touched me deeply. Pain is inextricably woven into the fabric of love. Can't you see its threads, thin and delicate, lying just beneath the surface? To isolate ourselves from pain is to isolate ourselves from true love, true happiness. It hurts so much when someone you love dies, because that person brought you so much happiness. "The pain now is part of the happiness then. That's the deal." Within that one line is the power to change a person's entire view of suffering, indeed, of life itself.

And could anyone other than Gregory Peck have given life to Atticus Finch as well as he did in *To Kill a Mockingbird*? Did his performance not somehow stir you to be a better person than you were before you saw it?

And what about *The Wizard of Oz*? Could any theological treatise be more compelling than Dorothy's words at the end of the movie? Remember the words she had to repeat as she clicked together her ruby slippers? Those words are what brought her back to her own bed in her own room in Kansas, where she was surrounded by the people she loved. Remember those words?

There's no place like home. There's no place like home.

Isn't that what the Prodigal Son said to himself, in essence, when he was starving in a distant country? Isn't that what we all say to ourselves when we walked away from God and experienced what life is like without Him? Isn't "There's no place like home" the winsome call of the gospel?

And then there's my favorite movie.

Camelot.

I was a young Christian when it first came out in 1969, and I had a lot of questions regarding the hows and whys of everything from creation to redemption. I knew Christ died for the sins of the world. What I didn't understand is why. Because he loved us, of course. I knew that. What I was unclear about was why the problem of humanity's sin couldn't be dealt with in another way? I mean, why couldn't God just forgive everyone with one sweeping judicial pardon? He was God, wasn't He? He could do whatever He wanted, couldn't He? But if for some reason He couldn't do that, why then couldn't He have just swept everyone away in judgment and simply start over again?

I can't remember specifically asking God to help me find an answer to that question, but maybe the Spirit of God translated those unspoken concerns into words and breathed them as a prayer on my behalf. Who knows? But dim the lights and draw the curtains, and I will show you what I saw in that theater in 1969.

Two of the greatest love stories ever told. The one, at Camelot; the other, at Calvary. Two of the noblest kings ever to live. The one, King Arthur; the other, King of the Jews. The one is adorned with a jeweled crown; the other, with a crown of thorns. The one is staged in elaborate settings and costumes with scenes of pomp and pageantry; the other, shrouded in darkness, with scenes of hair matted from dried blood, of wounds throbbing with fever, of bones disjointed from the pendulous slump of weight that did not resist. The one is poetically carried along by musical interludes; the other, prosed in broken fragments of conversations, punctuated by the guttered tauntings of a mob thirsting for blood. The one is a stage and film masterpiece, play and lyrics by Alan Jay Lerner, music by Frederick Loewe; the other, a dark page from history, written simply by a few inarticulate friends of the deceased.

The comparisons and contrasts between *Camelot* and Calvary are many, but one scene from *Camelot* illustrates a great theological dilemma that only the Cross could resolve. Was there no other path than the rocky incline that led to Calvary?

A King's Request Denied

Prior to his appointment with destiny on the brow of that fateful hill, Jesus agonized in the garden of Gethsemane: "Father, if you are willing, take this cup from me; yet not my will, but yours be done."

The emotional atmosphere surrounding those words is heavy with sweat and tears. The verses following tell of Jesus "being in agony" and "praying very fervently." So exhausting was the ordeal that afterward it was necessary for an angel to come and strengthen Him.

Understand, on an emotional level, that this is the pleading of a son to his father. If your child came to you in such agony, asking, begging, and pleading with such a submissive heart, wouldn't you do everything within your power to grant the request? "Which of you," Jesus himself taught, "if his son asks for bread, will give him a stone? Or if he asks for a fish, will give him a snake?" Wouldn't you give food to one of your children who came to you with such hunger? Certainly you would. "If you then, though you are evil, know how to give good gifts to your children, how much more will your Father in heaven give good gifts to those who ask him!"

But this Father, this time, didn't. And that's the theological rub. He denied the request of His Son, His only Son, His beloved Son. In Gethsemane that Son was asking: "Is there no other way?" The Father's answer is found in the paragraphs following the request. The Son is betrayed, arrested, deserted, denied, beaten, tried, mocked, and finally crucified. Tacitly the Father answers: "No, there is no other way."

Instead of the removal of suffering's cup, Jesus is given sour wine upon the cross. An apparent stone for the requested loaf. A snake for a fish.

But why? Why was there no other way?

The Execution Scene at Camelot

I found the answer to that question in a scene from *Camelot*, where the adulterous relationship between Queen Guenevere and Arthur's most trusted knight, Sir Lancelot, has divided the Round Table. When the scheming Mordred catches them in a clandestine encounter, Lancelot escapes. Guenevere is not so fortunate. The chorus sings her fate:

On a day, dark and drear,
Came to trial Guenevere.
Ruled the jury for her shame
She be sentenced to the flame.

As the day of execution nears, people come from miles around with one question in their minds:

Would the King let her die?
Would the King let her die?
There was wonder far and near:
Would the King burn Guenevere?

After the chorus posed the question, Mordred enters the scene:

Arthur! What a magnificent dilemma!
Let her die, your life is over;
Let her live, your life's a fraud.
Which will it be Arthur? Do you kill
the Queen or kill the law?

The fact that Arthur was Guenevere's husband, and, at the same time, her king, created the dilemma. If he carries out the sentence, he upholds the law and validates himself to be a just and impartial king. Yet, in doing so, he calls into question his love. "Would the King burn Guenevere?" His tender wife whom he affectionately called Jenny? Jenny, who gave sparkle to his eyes? Jenny, who gave joy to his heart?

His heart tells him to set her free. If he did, it would certainly remove any doubt of his love. But by bending justice and showing partiality, he would call into question his right to rule.

Tragically but resolutely, Arthur decides:

Treason has been committed! The jury has ruled!
Let justice be done!

The chorus continues:

She must burn. She must burn.
Spoke the king: She must burn.
And the moment now was here
For the end of Guenevere.

High from the castle window stands Arthur as Guenevere enters the courtyard. Accompanying her are two guards and a priest. She walks to her unlit stake, where the executioner stands with waiting torch. Arthur turns away, emotion brimming in his eyes, as the chorus continues:

Slow her walk, bowed her head,
To the stake she was led . . .

A herald mounts the tower where Arthur has withdrawn:

The Queen is at the stake, Your Majesty.
Shall I signal the torch?

Arthur is devastated. Again the herald calls, this time with greater urgency:

Your Majesty . . . ! Your Majesty . . . !

But the King cannot answer. In the background the chorus adds:

In his grief, so alone
From the King came a moan . . .

Arthur's love for Jenny spills from his broken heart:
I can't! I can't! I can't let her die!
Seeing Arthur crumble, Mordred relishes the moment:

Well, you're human after all, aren't you,
Arthur? Human and helpless.

Tragically, Arthur realizes the truth of Mordred's remark. Being only human, he is indeed helpless. But where this story ends, the greatest story ever told just begins.

The Execution Scene at Calvary

Another time. Another place. Another king.

The setting: A world lies estranged from the God who loves it. Like Guenevere, an unfaithful humanity stands guilty and in bondage, awaiting judgment's torch.

Could God turn His head from the righteous demands of the law and simply excuse the world's sin? If not, then could He turn His head from the world He loved? "Would the King burn Guenevere?"

Like the wicked Mordred, Satan must have looked on in delight:

God! What a magnificent dilemma!
Let them die, your life is over;
Let them live, your life's a fraud;
Which will it be God? Do you kill your
world or do you kill the law?

Without even waiting for his Guenevere to look up in repentance, this King stepped down from his throne, took off his crown, laid aside his royal robes, and descended his castle's polished steps into humanity's pockmarked streets. Paul's words in Philippians are thought by some scholars to be the lyrics of an ancient hymn, singing about the King of Kings . . .

Who, being in very nature God,
did not consider equality with God
something to be grasped,
but made himself nothing,
taking the very nature of a servant,
being made in human likeness.
And being found in appearance as a man,
he humbled himself,
and became obedient to death—
even death on a cross!

God became a man so that Jesus, unlike Arthur, would be neither simply human nor helpless. He stepped down from his throne, giving up the luxury of the castle to live on earth. We were his Guenevere. He was both our king and the lover of our soul. And He gave up his Camelot for our cross. When He did, God satisfied both His love for us and the righteous demands of His law.

For me that scene in the movie was an epiphany of understanding. Suddenly it all made sense. I knew now why he had to die, why there was no other way.

I learned that when I was a freshman in college.

Not from college.

Not even from seminary.

From a movie.

A Prayer for Moments

Help me, O God,

Whenever I go to a movie, not to go just for entertainment
*   but also for enlightenment.*
Meet me there, I pray, and speak to me.
Tell me something I need to know so I may live my life
*   more graciously, more compassionately.*
Give me moments of transcendence
*   so I can leave the theater in some way changed,*
*   even if it is a very small way.*
Speak to me through a character, a scene, a line of dialogue, a musical score,
Tell me something that will help me become
*   a more understanding person,*
*   kinder and more compassionate.*
Thank You for those moments at the movies
*   that have touched my heart.*
And for the fact that there is no place on earth
*   that some echo of Your voice cannot be heard*
*   for the one who is listening . . .*

Windows of Memory

If life is just a highway,
Then the soul is just a car,
And objects in the rear-view mirror
May appear closer than they are.

MEATLOAF
"Objects in the Rear-view Mirror"

Now matter how fast we drive or how far away, we can never escape our past. Even though it is behind us, it is always in our rear-view mirror. And though it seems that the images of our past should grow smaller, the irony is that the farther down life's highway we travel, the closer they sometimes appear. Always just a glance away. And always glancing back at us. The images in that mirror may send us safely on our way, or they may send us crashing into a ditch. Such is the power of memories.

Of those memories, none is more powerful than memories of home. We may leave home, but home never really leaves us. Deep inside all of us is something that draws us back. The reasons are as many as our memories.

Søren Kierkegaard once said: "Life must be lived forwards, but it can be understood only backwards." Maybe the reason we are drawn back home is a longing to understand what influences shaped us to be the way we are, think the way we do, act the way we do or react, feel the way we do or don't feel.

Or maybe we are drawn there because we long to experience what we can of the past while there's still time to do it, to go back and savor the meal life served up for us at the table of our youth, to taste it all once more, to chew longer on those things we gulped down so quickly, those things that filled us with such joy and peace and love.

Maybe we're drawn back there to see it all for what it all really was—a gift. An incredible, immeasurable gift to be cherished. Maybe one of the reasons we're drawn home is a need to give thanks for what we so casually received and took for granted.

Or maybe the reason we are drawn home is that there's unfinished business back there, something that's come to our attention in such a way that we can no longer look away. Maybe that unfinished business is a wound that needs healing or a wound we've inflicted on someone else that only we can heal. Maybe it's an offense that needs forgiving or one we've committed that needs to be forgiven us. Maybe there are words we need to say or words we need to hear. Maybe there is something we need to understand that per-haps all of our life we have misunderstood. Or maybe there is something about us someone else needs to understand. Whatever the reason, memories draw us home with gravitational force. It's a force we can resist, but only at the expense of our soul.

The older I get, the larger those things in the rear-view mirror appear. Sometimes they loom so large I have to stop the car and turn around and go back. Go back and see what the past is asking of me, requiring of me. Go back and see what I've forgotten, what I've inadvertently left behind. Go back to find it, pick it up, and attend to it. Only then can I continue down the road of my spiritual journey.

The road I've traveled has taken me a long way from my boyhood home. I have returned there many times, for many reasons. The reason that draws me there this time is an aunt with Alzheimer's.

But before I stop to see her, I stop somewhere else. I stop at the part of town where I spent the first ten years of my life.

The Westerner Drive-In behind our house is gone now. The field behind our backyard that once seemed to stretch forever in a tangle of scrub oak and wild ivy is now a tidily kept neighborhood of fast-food restaurants. The River Oaks Theater with its Saturday matinees is gone, too. The A. L. Davis Food Store is gone. The penny-candy store across from the elementary school is gone.

So is my father.

He and they remain in my mind, memories of them stored like bulbs in fertile ground, growing within me, waiting to blossom in ways I can't begin to imagine. But other things remain, other people remain, that I can still see, still touch, still hold on to.

My mother is still there, my brother, my sister. The elementary school is still there. The small snow-cone stand, it's still standing. I stop there and buy a dollar's worth of shaved ice in a paper cone, dripping with blue coconut syrup. It's good, but not as good as I remembered it thirty-five years ago when it was a nickel and I was a burr-headed boy walking home from school.

Across the street I see that school. It has weathered the years with little change. It has been repainted with the same glaring white it wore when I was a boy. It has not been remodeled, and it doesn't have the usual shanty town of temporary annexes most schools have. The playground is no longer the grassy field it once was but has been asphalted, striped with white paint for hopscotch, dodge ball, and four-square. I walk across the street and around back.

I look in the window of the cafeteria, where I ate for the first four grades of my educational life. Was it always this small? I look into another window, then another, looking for my old classroom. I arch my hands over my eyes, press my face to the glass.

There it is.

It is a small room with lockers lining the walls. The blackboards are crowned with an alphabetic border of flawless cursive script. The cast-iron radiator. Can't believe they still have that. I wonder if it still clanks when the steam spirits through its pipes? Images of boys come to mind, standing in line to use the pencil sharpener, each bringing with him a crayon to melt on that old radiator.

Thirty-five years. Has it been that long? Thirty-five years. It sounds like a long time. Somehow, though, it doesn't seem long. It all seems so vividly yesterday. The sultry cling of the heat. The smell of the freshly cut grass with what has always seemed to me to be a hint of watermelon hiding in it somewhere. The taste of the cold drippy funnel of snow that would freeze your brain if you ate it too fast, and I always ate it too fast.

I finish the cone, which this time I have eaten slowly, and I drive to the old neighborhood, whose trees are tall and leafy with the years but whose streets no longer teem with children. Instead they teem with memories.

I remember the dusky end of the day and running through the yards to catch lightning bugs. I remember packing a little white cardboard suitcase with a plastic handle and running away from home. Not as dramatic as it sounds. It was more like walking away from home. I got as far as a neighbor's house around the corner, and I came back that afternoon. I remember how we traded comic books and army men and trading cards, how we put up lemonade stands and threw together talent shows at a minute's notice.

Texas summers were full of bull nettles and sticker bushes and Johnson grass growing up like little corn stalks, except without the corn. The freshly graveled streets oozed tar that by the end of the day blackened your bare feet so thoroughly you had to scrub them down with a rag full of gasoline to get it off. The ground crawled with red ants and hopped with grasshoppers, and everywhere there were wart frogs and horned toads and slick, rainbow-colored lizards whose tails came off in your hand when you tried to catch them, flailing between your pinched fingers with a life of their own.

Days were spent waiting for Fourth of July, eating watermelon, and running through sprinklers. The highlight of each day was the Popsicle truck that made its rounds, poking along over the neighborhood streets, its carousel music piping over a scratchy speaker, sending kids scrambling for loose change, going through the house, the drawers, the bottoms of their mothers' purses, trying to scrape up enough pennies for an exotic-flavored Popsicle you couldn't get at the store, or, for a few pennies more, a Sidewalk Sunday.

I look down the street and on the corner I see the communal lamppost where we used to congregate after dark, sitting on the curb under the soft circumference of its light, waiting till a screen door swung open, when one by one our parents called us home, each call punctuated by the exclamation mark of a screen door slapping shut.

I ease on the brake as I come to the blonde brick house where I spent the first ten years of my life. A "For Rent" sign stands stiffly in the yard. It's empty. Nobody's there. A rush of boyish excitement comes over me.

I get out of the car and approach the house, looking at the carport my dad built and the garage he turned into a knotty pine bedroom. I step onto the porch, which seems so small to me now, and I try the door. It's locked. I go around and try the back door. Locked.

I look in every window. What is it I'm looking for? What is it I'm hoping to find?

Room by room the memories come back to me. It all went by so fast, or so it seems now as I stand there, looking in the windows. But to a barefoot boy sauntering through the summer months it seemed an entire geological age from Fourth of July until Christmas. Now, it seems a few turns around the face of a watch.

I look across the street at all the other houses, and suddenly, there we all are playing hide-and-seek in those front yards, biking around the block, playing sandlot ball on the vacant field, whose grass has long forgotten the feet that once played there and the stains it once put on our jeans as we slid into the bases.

During those days of endless play, I got into my share of mischief and naughty things, and the times I got caught red-handed or tattled on I got my mouth washed out with soap or a good switching or an oblique sermonette on how my body is the temple of the Holy Spirit. I also got into my share of fights, taking a fist now and then, and now and then landing one on someone else. But I never started a fight, never picked on someone or bullied someone, never went around looking to hurt someone.

Except once.

I was eight, I think, maybe nine. A friend and I were playing catch, and a kid named Reese from around the block wanted to horn in on our game. For some reason, which escapes me now, we didn't let him. But he kept at it, pushing to be included, and finally, we pushed back. We pushed him and hit him, and by the time it was all over we had split his lip and broken one of his permanent teeth. As he ran home crying, my friend and I laughed and congratulated ourselves with "That'll-teach-him" kind of talk.

A few minutes later his sister came running around the corner. She was older than we were and bigger, and as angry as she was she could have beaten the both of us up. She didn't. But through her tears she yelled at us and told us off and made me feel the way I should have felt all along— ashamed.

I vaguely remember—maybe because my parents got wind of it and made me, I don't know—going to his house later and apologizing. I hope I did, anyway.

I was not a bad boy. The boy I was playing catch with was not a bad boy. But together we did something terribly bad that to this day I terribly regret. It certainly wasn't the only bad thing I've ever done. Over the years I've done lots of things to keep it company. But this one thing in particular has lived within me like a shameful secret, cowering in the dark. And even though the years take me further away from that incident, it's still with me, looming larger in my rear-view mirror.

Not long after that, Reese moved. His father was in the Air Force so I suspect he moved a lot over the years, and I suspect that it was always difficult being the new kid on the block, trying to make friends with kids who had been friends with each other for years and didn't need any new kid horning in. Tick-tock, game's locked. It's a game we've all played, but it's a hurtful game to the one who gets locked out. I'm sure it wasn't easy for Reese growing up, adjusting to new schools, new neighborhoods, new friends, and I hadn't made it any easier.

As for me, my father wasn't in the Air Force, but over a period of forty-five years I have moved a total of ten times. With each move a little of my past gets thrown away or given away, put in a garage sale or carted off to the Goodwill. Few things have survived all ten of those moves, and almost nothing from my old neighborhood.

Except this.

A letter from Reese.

He had sent it to me after he moved, and it resurfaced thirty-five years later as I was getting ready to move myself, this time from California to Colorado.

March 16, 1961
Dear Kenny
    I feel like going back to Fort Worth when I think of you. After I get through writing you I'm going to write our room. Hope you're OK. They won't let us play baseball at school. Tell the class I said I miss every one of them. Today at school they made us go out in the rain. Later today it snowed and it was the coldest day we've had since we arrived. I've got to go now.
    Sincerely,
    Reese

I beat him up.

"Dear Kenny."

I broke one of his permanent teeth.

"I hope you're OK."

And I laughed about it.

"Sincerely, Reese."

Who knows but that the soldiers who put Christ on the cross needed to hear the words He spoke, maybe not then but certainly someday when they looked back with terrible regret at the terrible bad they had done that brutal day on that brutal hill with their tight circle of friends.

"Father,"

Jesus prayed, as the soldiers played their game, gambling for His garment.

"Forgive them,"

he asked, as they laughed and cursed and felt no shame.

"For they know not what they do."

In those words was the forgiveness those soldiers desperately needed, although they didn't know it at the time. Between the lines in Reese's letter, there was forgiveness too, forgiveness I desperately needed. I didn't know it then. I do now.

Life is more than just a highway, as the song goes, and the soul is more than simply a car, but some objects in the rear-view mirror really do appear larger than they are. And sometimes it takes a word of forgiveness to reduce them to size and keep them from overwhelming us. For me that word came in the form of a letter, a letter handed me at a window of the soul. "I forgave you a long time ago," God seemed to be saying, "and I just wanted you to know that Reese did too."

I hope to run into Reese someday, tell him how sorry I was for what I did. But if I don't, I hope God has preserved a note I wrote him or a school picture I gave him or a good memory I might have left him, something, anything, to let him know how I feel.

The really beautiful thing about all this is that God knew, I think, how years later I would regret what I had done. And I think He knew what it would take to resolve that regret—some tangible evidence, something I could touch and hold in my hand, something to let me know Reese had forgiven me.

A letter, maybe.

I left the old neighborhood, taking with me a leaf from a tree my father planted in the front yard. I remember when he planted it. It was so small I used to get a running start and jump over it. Now it towers over me. It had grown up.

And, by the grace of God, so had I.

I left the old neighborhood and drove to another part of town where my aunt lived. I came to see her, thinking it would probably be the last time I would see her before she died. Her husband greeted me at the door and invited me in. And there she was. I hardly recognized her.

She was in a wheelchair, wearing a faded housedress. Her hair was gray and stringy; her muscles, atrophied; her skin, like a baby bird's, thin and translucent to where you could see the embroidery of her veins. She was frail and looked as if she would break if you hugged her. I hugged her, and she didn't. But she didn't recognize me either. She babbled incoherently, repeating a series of syllables. I tried talking to her, telling her that Judy and the kids said hello and give her their best, but she just mumbled on, the same syllables going round and round like a warped record stuck in a groove.

She was my father's sister, and the only one in their family still alive. When she dies, she will take the family's entire history with her. When she dies, there will be no one left to tell the family's stories, what it was like growing up in Kansas during the Depression, what my dad was like when he was little, what joys they experienced, what tragedies they endured. She was the last one who knew these things, remembered these things. One by one, the others who remembered had died. Heart attack. Stroke. Heart attack.

Now Alzheimer's.

That was the worst, I think. Forgetting not simply where you put your glasses or car keys, but forgetting where you've been and where you are, forgetting who you are and once were, whom you loved and who loved you.

Her husband and daughter wheeled her into the other room and lifted her into bed. When they returned, we talked about her condition and what the doctors were doing for her or not doing, what medication she was taking and how she was reacting to it, what kind of diet she was on, things like that. She couldn't do anything for herself. Couldn't dress herself, feed herself, bathe herself. She was like a baby, only a baby that weighed something like ninety pounds, which made dressing her and bathing her and putting her to bed an exhausting ordeal. Her babbling was like a baby's too, except at times the tone was insistent, even angry. She was declining fast and would have to be put in a nursing home, they told me.

When time came for me to leave, I went into the bedroom to say my last good-bye to an aunt who all of her life had loved me but who now no longer even knew me.

I touched her hand and stroked the soft, slack skin on her arm. "I have to leave now," I told her, trying to get her attention over the babbling. And as I reached down to hug her, the babbling stopped. "I love you," I said as I kissed her forehead. Her frail, slack arms reached up to me, trembling with weakness, and she tried the best she could to hug me and said, "I love you too."

She remembered who I was. Maybe only for a moment, but she remembered.

As I got into my car, tears pooled in my eyes. So this is how it all ends. This is how we slip out of this world, with all the limitations of a baby but with none of its loveliness. Every day losing a little bit of our motor skills and a little bit of our minds. Every day losing more of our balance and losing more control of our bowels. Every day losing a little something else until at last there's little else to lose except life itself.

No wonder relatives want to shield us from seeing loved ones who get like this. But I wanted to see this aunt whom I loved and who loved me, see her one last time, even if it meant seeing her like this.

"It is better to go to a house of mourning than to go to a house of feasting," said Solomon, "for death is the destiny of every man; the living should take it to heart." There is a window in that house of mourning, is what Solomon in essence is saying, and in that window is a wisdom we can't find anywhere else. In that window is a truth so frightening we do everything we can to keep from looking at its face, and everything we can to shield others from looking at it.

The truth is, that is the way of all flesh. The truth is, that person in the wheelchair who babbles on and can't remember will be me someday if I live long enough. Or it will be someone I love. My mother, maybe. Or maybe my wife.

It seems so sad that it all comes down to this. Oh, I know, I know there's a resurrection. I know we get new bodies. I know that death will be defeated, that all our tears will be wiped away. I know all that, I believe all that. But knowing all that and believing all that didn't make that day any less sad for me, didn't take away the sick feeling I got in the pit of my stomach, didn't take away the depression I felt at the futility of it all, or the anger I felt at seeing a whole life wearing down to a housedress of flesh and bones that can't remember.

But it wasn't death that bothered me that day. It wasn't even the debilitating effects of getting old. It was the obliteration of memory. To have all that history erased. All those birthdays and Christmases and family vacations. All the laughter, all the tears, all the love that was shared, the words that were spoken, all that was given and received, all of it gone. Every bit of it gone. That was the tragedy.

"I love you."
"I love you too."

All of the gospel is in those words. And that is the other window I saw. For you and I have lost our memory, forgotten who we are and who it is that loves us. Yet even in our forgetfulness, God has not forgotten us. He reaches down to embrace us, to kiss us on the forehead and tell us, "I love you." The best we can do is remember for a moment who we are and, even if it's for the briefest of moments, remember who it is that loves us, reach up with our palsied arms, respond with our faltering voice, and say, "I love you too."

"I love you" is a pretty accurate translation of the words God spoke through the Cross.

"I love you too" is not too far a translation of the thief's response when he said, "Remember me when you come into your kingdom," when, for the briefest of moments, and maybe for the first time in his life, he remembered who he was and who it was that loved him.

A Prayer for Remembrance

Help me, O God,

To understand that when objects in the rear-view mirror appear larger than
*   they are,*
*   they appear that way not to intimidate me*
*   but to get my attention.*
Help me to understand that those images looming in my memory
*   are just trying to get me to stop, turn around, and go back to my past,*
*   to pick up something that's back there,*
*   something that is essential for the journey I am on,*
*   something I need if I am to go on any farther.*
Help me to remember the love I have received along the way,
*   and to be remembered for the love I have given.*
Help me to understand how short that journey is,
*   and slow me down so I don't pass any of it by.*
And if you grant me the grace of a long life,
*   grant me the greater grace*
*   to always remember who I am*
*   and who it is that loves me . . .*

Windows of Dreams

For God does speak—now one way, now another—
though man may not perceive it.
In a dream, in a vision of the night,
when deep sleep falls on men
as they slumber in their beds. . . .

JOB 33:14–16

Sometimes it's the middle of the night when God opens a window. And when He does, sometimes what He shows us is a picture. Why a picture? When you hear Al and Patty's story, I think you'll understand why.

The story begins in 1982, when Al and Patty were married. Like all newlyweds, their eyes were filled with stars and their hearts with dreams of happily-ever-aftering. Al was rising in the ranks of the Air Force and working toward becoming an expert on the Soviet Union. Following a master's degree in Soviet affairs, he pursued a Ph.D. in the same field with his sights set on a career serving his country in the Soviet Union. Patty had the same dream, and along with Al she worked diligently on becoming fluent in Russian. She also dreamed of having a house full of children.

But three years later those dreams began to die.

Al was diagnosed with multiple sclerosis. The disease eats away the protective lining around the nerve tissue, like mice gnawing on the insulation around the electrical wiring in a house. Circuit by circuit the nervous system shorts out and shuts down. Over the next nine years, Al went from being a cross-country runner to walking with a cane, from a promising military career to no career at all.

Within a year of Al's diagnosis, Patty began her own downward spiral. Beginning with varied and seemingly unrelated health problems, her body was starting to short-circuit too. Finally, the diagnosis came in. *Systemic Lupus.* A progressive, incurable disease of the auto-immune system. During the first twelve months following her diagnosis, she had thirteen different infections, ranging from infections of the sinuses to the lymph glands. Her muscles constantly ache and her joints have deteriorated arthritically from the disease. She wakes up every morning feeling like the Tin Man in *The Wizard of Oz* with his rusty joints. But for her, there is no oil can nearby to give her relief.

Al and Patty grieve for all the losses in their lives, the loss of health, loss of career, loss of a family. And they fear, understandably, all the losses yet to come. The loss of mobility. The loss of memory. The loss of a mate. And who knows what others?

But they are neither angry nor disillusioned. They are in fact two of the most delightful people you would ever want to be around. One of the reasons for that is their belief in a sovereign God. They prayed, of course, that He would sovereignly take it all away. Take away the pain. Take away the debilitating effects of the disease. The disease itself. But He hasn't. So their Gethsemane prayers for the removal of that cup turned to ones resigning themselves to receive it. Even though the cup was hard to take, they believed it came from their Father's hand, a hand that was good and that had a purpose for all their pain.

Their pain mounted when Al's health took a sharp turn for the worse, and he became unable to continue working. During this time he read the story of the Prodigal Son, which he had read many times before, but now, as he read it in his quiet time, it took on new significance. He shared with Patty how the story had touched him, how overwhelmed he had been by the father's compassion, how touched he had been by his tears and by the way he embraced his son, throwing his arms around him, restoring him to his former status with a son's robe and ring and sandals, killing the fatted calf for him and throwing a party in his honor.

What touched Al most about the story was the father's compassion. The son came home only to avoid starvation, but what he found when he returned was more than a hot meal, more than a mere servant's position within his father's house, more in fact than what he hoped for in his wildest expectations. As Al reflected on the passage, he realized that the son received this unbelievable future and hope only because of the father's overwhelming compassion for him.

While Al wasn't a prodigal, he did have fears about how Patty and he would survive now that neither of them could work. How would they eat? Where would they live? How would they get by?

Al had no idea how these questions would be resolved, but he had a very clear idea who would resolve them, and he was certain that the only way to face their uncertain future was to cling to a compassionate God and rest in His embrace.

It was such a beautiful picture, the picture of the father's embrace, and one Al longed to see. He never doubted God's presence, but he longed to see Him, hear Him, sense His compassion, feel His touch. Now more than ever.

For a month they prayed to see a glimpse of their heavenly Father, a nod of the head, a wink of the eye, the slightest of smiles, anything. Sometimes Patty would cry for thirty minutes before she could even say the simple words, "God help us. Have compassion on us."

By now Christmas was approaching. Patty's favorite time of the year. But now she and Al were too weak to even bring out the boxes of decorations. Knowing how much the season meant to Patty, several friends gave her and Al a small Christmas tree decorated with red bows, each bow wrapped around a twenty-dollar bill. Patty broke down and wept. Another friend called offering round-trip tickets and an invitation to spend Christmas with them by Monterey Bay at Pebble Beach, California. They left, taking with them the tree's harvest for their spending money.

While they were there, they were treated like royalty. They felt so special, so loved. As they were walking along the Monterey Wharf, their friend suggested stopping at a nearby art gallery. As they entered, Patty's eyes were drawn to the middle of the room where a light from the ceiling funneled down upon a piece of sculpture. She and Al walked toward it, amazed.

It was the Prodigal Son being embraced by his father.

The son was clutching his father's coat as tears streamed down the father's face.

The image of that father embracing his son had become a part of Al and Patty's emotional vocabulary, and God reached into the language of their soul, using that image to tell them things they desperately needed to hear.

"Yes, I hear your prayers," is what they sensed God saying through that sculpture. "Yes, I am a compassionate God.

"And yes, I love you."

They stood before that sculpture, stunned and silent. But they stood wrapped in His arms, clutching His coat with their tears.

Certainly God speaks through words but so often, as in Al and Patty's story, it seems He speaks without them. Not because He can't speak or because we can't hear, but because words are often the least effective way of communicating.

No one knows that more, I think, than a writer. What words, for example, do you use to describe the fragrance of a rose? So common. So familiar to us all. But what words *do* you use? What words do you use to express all that is in your heart when you fell in love? Remember those feelings? Can you find words to match those feelings? And when God flooded your life in a way that forever changed your life, what words do you use to describe the experience in a way that does not diminish the experience to those you're describing it to?

Whatever words we use, something is always lost in the translation. That is especially true of the words we use in trying to describe God.

I could use words to describe God's power or show you a jeweler's treasure flung across the black velvet of a moonless sky. Which communicates more clearly, a word like "majestic" or simply the sight of the Milky Way? I could find dictionary words to answer the question "Who is my neighbor?" or show you a picture of the Good Samaritan. Which is more vivid? I could read a psalmist's hymn describing God's undying love, or show you God's love dying on a cross. Which is more compelling, the words or the picture?

The person who said a picture is worth a thousand words was saying, in essence, how devalued words are in the currency exchange between souls. They are worth only pennies on the dollar in their power to purchase a description of the experiences of the soul.

I have words from my wife that she has written in notes, letters, and anniversary cards and memories of words she that has spoken in conversations, but I also have recollections of her that have no words.

I have pictures, for example, taken of her at Christmas and vacations and birthdays. I have memories of the German pancakes she surprises me with from time to time, knowing how much I enjoy them. I have thrift-store books she has bought me over the years, thinking they were ones I didn't have and might want, letting me know in ways I understand that I was somewhere in her thoughts as she went about her day.

Through all of these things something of her love is expressed. Reflect a moment on how you express your love. Do you do it through words? Certainly. Only through words? No. You send flowers, maybe, with a note attached. Or maybe to enhance the mystery, you don't attach a note. You hold the person's hand or embrace the person or rub the stress from the person's shoulders. Maybe you plan a special evening, or a surprise party, or pick out a special gift, a gift so timely and so personal that the very giving of it reveals the intimacy of the relationship.

Through these varied and often unspoken ways something of your love is voiced. That something may say, "I miss you," or "I know you're under a lot of stress and I understand," or "I thought about you today and I just wanted you to know."

Why should the way God voices His love be any different?

In the Old Testament when God spoke to Joseph through a dream, He used images that were familiar to him, images of the field where he and his brothers had worked. When He spoke in a dream to the king's cupbearer in prison, He used an image of grapes. When He spoke to the king's baker, He used an image of bread. Because all of these images were so familiar to the recipients, each sensed God was speaking to him directly.

God spoke to those people then and speaks to us now in the language most familiar to us. I'm not talking about our native language, with all its regional dialects and colloquialisms. I'm talking about the language of our heart. And not the human heart in general, but each individual heart, with its own intensely personal images.

For Al and Patty that image was the father's embrace. For you and me, those images most likely will be different, for each of us over a lifetime has compiled our own dictionary of emotionally rich vocabulary. Some of the images are dark, and a mere glimpse of them makes us shudder. Others are bright and colorful and bring sparkle to our eyes. Still others bring tears.

Skim through the pages of your past and you'll find a few of your own. Maybe one of them is the cuddly feel of grandma's quilt. Or the familiar smell of a lumpy teddy bear. Your mother in the kitchen baking cookies, maybe. Or a tree house. Your father putting shingles on the roof. The creosote pole of the streetlight you sat under so many summer nights ago before your parents called you in from play. A tag-along dog that kept you company. A limp rag doll that kept your secrets. All these images are words from the language of your heart.

My wife and I were going through a time in our own spiritual journey where we longed to hear words like that, words to let us know our Father in heaven had been watching us grow up over the years, that He had seen our skinned knees and nightmares and high temperatures, that He had been watching out for us and was watching out for us still.

He had spoken to His children in times past, and we heard echoes of His voice in the Scriptures, but we longed to hear Him speaking not to Moses or to David but to us, directly, personally, intimately.

No communication is as intimate I think as a dream whispered to our soul in the middle of the night. I didn't always think that, though. Mainly because most of the dreams I've had over the years have bubbled up from the fears or desires cauldroned within my subconscious. You know, the ones where you're in class and suddenly realize you've got nothing on but your underwear. Or you're in bed and a robber's hiding in your closet and you're screaming to your parents down the hall except no words are coming out and the robber's coming to get you and despite your efforts to jump out of bed and run your body is a sack of concrete and he's coming closer and you can't even pull the covers over your head and you scream louder but still no words are coming out. Those kinds of dreams.

I used to put people who talked about God speaking to them in dreams in the same category as palm readers. At best, I thought them suspect. At worst, downright spooky. And if I ever got cornered by one at a party or somewhere, I'd gulp down my drink and go darting for the nearest punch-bowl. I used to think that way about a person who dreamed.

Until that person was my wife.

The dream she had was set in a huge gymnasium. Windows lined the top of the thirty-foot walls, letting in diffused rays of sunlight. She was sitting on the floor with a young man she didn't recognize but somehow felt she knew. The two of them were watching a ballet where hundreds of beautiful dancers in soft gowns were dancing. It was the most wonderful dance she had ever seen. Though her body wasn't moving, everything inside her was caught up in the dance and she felt part of it, one with it, and it filled her senses so fully she felt she would never tire of it.

The young man stood up and walked to the center of the gym. As he did, the ballerinas all bowed before him and floated on their toes to the far walls. Then he made an announcement: "Now I want *her* to dance."

Judy realized he was talking about her.

She got up and walked to where he was standing. Once by his side, she realized she was wearing grubby-looking workout clothes with torn leggings. But her concern was only momentary. When the young man left the center of the floor and sat down to watch, she began to dance. She swung her leg up high, turning her body in the opposite direction as she did, and then danced to the end of the gym. Each time she reached one end, she swung her foot high in the air, pivoted on the other foot, turned and danced to the other end.

Then, as quickly as she started dancing, she stopped and sat down beside the young man. He walked to the center of the gym and addressed the ballerinas: "See how beautifully she dances. She has had no training, yet see how she dances. I love her dance."

As little Judy left the gym floor, the ballerinas resumed their places, and the ballet continued. The young man took her aside and showed her a photo album filled with pictures of a beautiful house. The rooms were lavish and the furnishings exquisite. As she marveled over them, he said: "This is my home. I want you to make your home there and dance for me."

When Judy woke from the dream, she couldn't understand it. It was so vivid in her memory, yet so vague in its meaning. She knew God had spoken in the past to people through dreams. Both Old and New Testaments were full of such accounts. But did He still? She didn't know.

She got dressed and took the kids to school with little thought of the dream. After she finished her morning routine, though, she was driving home, and the dream came back to her. Vividly came back to her. As she was watching herself dance, her thoughts were interrupted by memories she had long since forgotten. Memories of when she was a young girl.

During her growing-up years when it was her turn to do dishes, Judy would dawdle at the sink. She would dip a dish into the soapy water, blow a bubble, think about something a minute, wash the dish, play with the water, think about something else, rinse the dish. And sometimes this would go on all evening until the dishes were done.

But when no one was around, young Judy would leave the dishes and dance back and forth from the kitchen to the living room. Each time she would come to the end of the room, she would swing one foot high in the air, pivot on the other foot, turn, and dance to the other end.

When that memory came back to her, a flood of tears came with it, tears for the little girl who carried so much sadness within her, never letting it come to the surface, never telling anyone her dreams or her heartaches.

Then suddenly it dawned on her.

The young man in the dream. It was Jesus. He had been there, watching her dance in that living room during those painful years of growing up. He knew her longings to be a ballerina. He knew she had no training. Knew she had to drop out of college to go to work. Knew the feelings of inadequacy she held so fragilely within her. Feelings that she was nobody special, that her life didn't matter, that other people could teach the Bible but not her, that good things happened to other people but not to her, that other people had interesting lives but not her.

Yet Jesus wanted *her*. Out of all the ballerinas, he picked *her* to dance for him, picked *her* to come to his house. It didn't make any difference that she didn't have any training or that she didn't have the lovely outfits the other ballerinas had. She had the heart of a ballerina. And she loved to dance. Those were the things that mattered.

Judy called me at work to tell me about the dream, not knowing how I would react but needing to tell me because it was such a beautiful dream and had touched her so deeply.

"So," I said, after she finished, "are you saying you want ballet lessons?"

"It's not about ballet," she said. "It's His way of telling me that He was there. Back then, when I was younger. He saw me. Nobody else saw me, but *He* saw me. I think, I don't know, but I think the dream was about Him being pleased with me and about His delight in my worship of Him, and I think He's inviting me into a more intimate relationship with Him."

I tried not to sound skeptical, for even over the phone I could tell how much the dream had meant to her, the emotion in her voice kept breaking the surface. After I hung up, I thought about it a few minutes. It was all so foreign to me. And yet there was no one in the world I respected more than Judy, no one whose heart I trusted more. She was not one to exaggerate or one who was prone to extremes. And she was not emotional. Yet she couldn't talk about the dream without tears.

I remember praying before I left work for God to help me understand. If indeed this was His voice, I didn't want to squelch it. If it wasn't, I didn't want to encourage it. I was driving home with these thoughts when I stopped at a Salvation Army Thrift Store, where I usually stopped once or twice a week, looking for used books. As I looked, my eye caught the spine of a slender book, titled, *A Dream So Real*. I remember thinking, *Odd coincidence*. I pulled the book off the shelf, and it fell open to a picture of a little girl on one page and a poem on the other. The little girl had her leg raised, as if trying to dance. And the poem? "Dream Dancer."

Was this the answer? So soon? Was God meeting me in a thrift store and telling me, yes, it's true, yes, it was me, it was my voice? I bought the book and brought it home, told Judy what I had prayed when I got off the phone, and I read her the poem. Again, she wept. Especially at the stanza which read:

Step then
from the staid and somber line.
Move out in dancing
into dreams so daring;
without them you will settle for the road
that wanders by and winds to nowhere.

For three days Judy cried, the emotions at times seeping to the surface, at other times surging with irrepressible force. After those three days, the tears were gone. And miraculously, so were the hurts from her past. Just like that. And they haven't come back.

Do you see what God was doing?

He paged through my wife's dog-eared dictionary of childhood memories, picked out an image that was dear to her, and one night bent down and whispered it in her ear. That image touched her in places where words alone couldn't reach. And with that touch, brought healing.

Look deeper into that picture. Do you see the window?

Do you see the ways of God revealed in the way He speaks? He didn't require Judy to go to seminary and learn Hebrew, the language through which He first spoke to His people. Instead, He learned hers.

He learned the language of her heart, which He had been studying since she was a girl. And it's a different language than He used when He spoke to Al and Patty. And still a different one than He uses when speaking to you and to me. Can you see how incredible that is?

Imagine the king of the Roman Empire, ruling over all the provinces in his far-reaching kingdom. Each with their own language, their own distinct dialect, their own regional colloquialisms. Now imagine him not requiring that the provinces learn Latin so they can converse with him but instead him learning the language of each individual province. Every dialect. Every colloquialism. Every regional metaphor. And he does this so he can speak to them personally in the language they most clearly understand.

It is hard to imagine the king of a great empire humbling himself like that. Even more so, the sovereign of the universe.

But that is what God does when He speaks to us through the images that are most dear to us. He picks images that are as indigenous to our world as a calculator is to the world of an accountant or as crayons are to the world of a kindergartner. The images may be so personal as to mean little, if anything, to anyone else. But they mean everything to us. He searches our heart for just the right image, as a mother would search her child's toy box for just the right stuffed animal that would dry the child's tears and bring a smile to the child's face.

That is how well He knows us.

And how much he loves us.

❧　❧

At night, when I tuck my kids in bed, sometimes I tell them a story, which is usually about when I was little or when they were. Sometimes I rub away the growing pains from their legs or the gardening pains from their backs. Sometimes I pray with them. Sometimes I don't say anything. I just sit on the bedside, looking in their eyes, hoping they will see the love in them and the delight. Sometimes I brush my hand across their face, kiss them on the cheek, tell them I love them and why. And maybe the way God speaks to us is not terribly far off from the way we speak to our children.

There have been moments in all of our lives when we've experienced God's voice. We may not have understood it, but we sensed Him speaking, sensed it was our name He was calling. Some of those moments may have been in dreams. In some of those dreams, He tells us a story maybe, or maybe rubs away the growing pains in our soul. Or He may tell us how proud He is to be our Father. A kid needs to hear that. A lot. He tells us that often throughout the day, but sometimes bedtime is the best time to hear it, when all the toys are put up and the books are back on the shelves and the spirit is still.

In some of those dreams, God counsels us, as any wise father would when his children are confused. In others, He shakes us, as any good father would when his children are in danger. Still other times, God stops by our room in the middle of the night, tucks the covers up around our chin, kisses us on the forehead, and in our ear whispers something that to a sleepy ear sounds a lot like "I love you." The way he did with Al and Patty one day. The way He did with Judy one night.

Those are the best dreams, the ones we never want to wake up from. And one day we won't.

One day, all of this life will seem to have been the dream, as all of Dorothy's adventures in Oz seemed when she found herself in her own bed, surrounded by the people who loved her, waking with the words on her lips: "There's no place like home. . . . There's no place like home."

One day we will feel a hand brushing across our cheek and a voice calling our name, and our eyes will open, as if from a long sleep, and on our bedside we will see Him whom we have longed all of our lives to see. And then we will realize, maybe for the first time . . .

that He was not only there when we woke up in the morning, but He was with us all through the night.

A Prayer for Insight

Help me, God,

To have insight into the nocturnal language of the soul,
with wide variety of images and richly textured emotions.
I am only a child, O God,
and I know so little of the love You have for me,
so little of the plans You have for me,
so little of the hopes and dreams,
fears and concerns.
Give me insight into all the feelings You have for me,
for though I am only a child,
I am Your child,
and I long to feel the covers as You tuck them under my chin,
sense Your touch as you kiss me goodnight,
and hear Your voice as You whisper Your love
in the sleepy ear of my soul . . .

Windows of Writing

"You should be writing something from your life, from the depths of your soul. There is more in you than this," he said, pointing to the newspaper story, *"if you have the courage to write it."*

LOUISA MAY ALCOTT
From the film adaptation of Little Women

The main character in *Little Women* is Jo, who goes to New York to follow her dream of becoming a writer. After she submits one of her stories to a newspaper editor, that dream is taken by the lapels and the smoke of a stubby cigar blown in its face.

"Our subscribers are not interested in sentiment and fairy stories, Miss," he said gruffly.

Jo frowned. "It isn't a fairy story."

"Try one of the ladies' magazines," he replied.

Jo stomped off, determined to do whatever she had to do to succeed. She didn't care how gruff the editors were or how offensive their cigars, she was determined to make a living at what she loved. Even if it killed her. So instead of writing stories she felt passionately about, she wrote stories she thought would sell. One day she received a letter from the same editor she had walked out on. He liked her story and wanted to publish it. She was ecstatic. In her excitement she rushed over to a new acquaintance of hers who had been at one time a professor of literature.

"The newspaper has taken two stories, and they wish to see more!" she said breathlessly.

"Wonderful!" he said. "May I?" He took the stories she held in her hand and began to read. Slowly, his happy expression changed to one of disappointment. "'The Sinner's Corpse' by Joseph March. You use another name?"

Jo nodded.

"They pay well I suppose?"

Jo felt angry and crushed at the same time. Why didn't he like what she had written? "People's lives are dull. They want thrilling stories," she said, her voice quavering.

The professor frowned. "People want whiskey, but I think you and I do not care to sell it." He cleared his throat and tapped the page with his finger. "This is a waste of your mind. You write of lunatics and vampires!"

"It will buy firewood for Marmee and Father, and a new coat for Beth, and she'll be grateful to have it," Jo said angrily. Tears filled her eyes. She grabbed the story and turned away. The professor gently took her arm to keep her from leaving.

"Please," he said. "I do not wish to insult you. Understand me. I am saying, you must please yourself. You must write about what you know, about what is important to you. I can see you have talent."

"You can?"

"Yes, but you should be writing something from your life, from the depths of your soul. There is more to you than this," he said, pointing to the newspaper story, "if you have the courage to write it."

Their conversation was an echo of one I had with God years ago when I was also an aspiring writer, also determined to make a living at what I loved, even if it killed me. The echo came from the small east Texas town of Nacogdoches where I had cut my teeth as a writer. Nothing I was writing at that time was selling, and things were getting desperate. More accurately, *I* was getting desperate.

It was then I came across an article in the Houston paper advertising a seminar for writing romance novels. "Send your money, come to Houston, and you too can become a successfully published author." The words dripped with honey too sweet to resist.

I went to a bookstore and surreptitiously bought one of the slender paperbacks, just to check it out. It took a couple of hours to read; how long could it take to write? A couple of weeks, a month maybe? What could I lose? How many months had I already lost with my own projects? What was one more?

So I sent my money, went to Houston, and spent a day listening as writers gave seductive testimonials and editors walked us through the do's and don'ts of writing formula romance. It was paint-by-the-numbers art, and on top of that, it was somebody else's numbers, but it was honest work and, who knows, it might buy firewood for Marmee and a coat for Beth.

I titled my story, *A More Congenial Spot*, from a line in a song from *Camelot*. I decided to write under a pseudonym. *It would need to be a woman's name*, I thought, something enticing, maybe something like that ad campaign for the perfume *Jontue*. Remember? "*Jontue* . . . Sensual, but not too far from innocence."

Now what name would that be?

Jessica. Sounds pretty sensual to me. Now how about the innocent part? Jones? Nice alliteration, but no, too common. Johnson? Too stable. Needs to have an exotic feel to it. St. John? Hmm. Jessica St. John. That's it!

Man, is this gonna be easy or what?

I spent a day brainstorming ideas and started getting really excited. Jessica would make a bundle, give it to Ken, Ken would take the bundle and use it to write something he really cared about.

I thought it best not to tell Judy about Jessica.

At least, not until the bundle changed hands.

She was visiting Fort Worth with the kids and called me, asking me how the writing was going. In the course of the conversation Jessica's name slipped out. I knew then I had to come clean about my literary tryst. Although Judy didn't discourage me, I detected a tinge of disappointment in her voice.

The next morning I read over what I had written, and each page became a window showing me something. Was it something about me? No, it was about Jessica, not about me. It wasn't *my* story, not really. It was what people wanted to read. People's lives are dull. They want thrilling stories. What harm was it in simply giving them what they wanted? It was honest money. It wasn't drugs, wasn't prostitution.

Or was it?

The French writer Molière once said, "Writing is like prostitution. First you do it for love, then you do it for a few friends, and finally you do it for money."

Was I?

Was what I did wrong? All I can say is, it was wrong for me.

It was a wrong turn at the crossroads between the survival of the body and the survival of the soul. Too many wrong turns and one day you or

I might wake up wondering where we are, how we ever ended up *here*, so far from what we once so passionately loved, so far from who we once were and once thought we would become. And one day we wake up and look at ourselves in the mirror and realize we have nothing to say anymore. What's worse, we don't even care.

Every day each of us comes to similar crossroads. In our thought life, our social life, or spiritual life, our professional life, in our life as a husband or a father, as a mother or a wife, as a son or a daughter, brother or sister, friend or neighbor. And every day we have to decide which way we're going to turn. Love and money are two roads that often intersect our path. Love of truth and the expedient safety of a lie are two others. Love thy neighbor and a got-to-get-to-Jericho schedule are two more.

Love is often the long way around to get to where we are going. But I have come to believe it is the right way around, and in taking it I don't think we can go too far wrong.

But this I didn't love. I didn't love the story or the characters or the whole cheapening experience of being seduced by such a drop-handkerchief kind of mistress. And so at page sixty-eight I stopped.

That I stopped writing the book said something about me, I thought. Something in my defense. That I started it in the first place said something too. Something I'm not sure I wanted to hear.

Whether we write formula romances or a thoughtful note to a friend or a few infrequent "Dear Diary" entries, what we write is a window into who we are. For humility's sake I saved the manuscript, every now and then taking it out of my files, dusting it off, and taking a good look at who I was not too many years ago.

My face still flushes with embarrassment each time I look at the manuscript with its white-shouldered margins yellowing with age and its smudgy type that looks like morning-after mascara. I get even more embarrassed when someone else looks at it. But I felt compelled to show you as I hope you will feel compelled to look, because all that is shown us at windows of the soul is not pretty to look at, and all that is told us is not pleasant to hear.

The heroine in the book is a woman who meets her romantic interest in a library, and the following paragraph describes their first encounter.

As she bent down, she saw through the space between the top of the books and the next shelf, the tawny slacks of the man she had just glimpsed. She froze, though she hardly knew why. Her heart began to pound within her. He stopped a moment as if perusing the shelf on the other aisle. His masculine cologne pushed its way through the books and took her senses off guard. She breathed in its fragrance and gently closed her eyes to the intimidating scent. Suddenly she became aware of her own fragrance, and she wondered if her perfume had met his nostrils. And if it had, she wondered, though she knew not why, if it had the same effect on him. She felt like a little girl hiding among the books. She would tell herself later, *how silly*, but for now his cologne clouded her thoughts.

Kinda makes you wanna puke, doesn't it? All that masculine cologne muscling its way through the aisles of a public library. Intimidating unsuspecting women. Sending their hearts pounding, eyelids closing, thoughts clouding . . . though they know not why. Sheesh. How clouded were my thoughts when I wrote that?

Not clouded enough to keep them from asking me some pretty soul-searching questions. Thoreau warned that "a man had better starve at once than lose his innocence in the process of getting his bread." Was that the cost I was paying—my innocence? Is this what I had worked so hard for, sacrificed so much for? If I was going to die trying to make a living at writing, I didn't want it to be here, no matter how congenial the spot. If I was going to die, it was going to be for something I loved, not for some street-corner flirtation.

My life as a writer started with writing children's books. *A More Congenial Spot* was the first book for an adult reader that I started. The first one I finished was *Intimate Moments with the Savior*. The project came to me two years after my fling with formula romance. I was working in California, co-authoring Bible study guides, when the printer sent us the final copy of the page layout before it went to press.

We got the copy in the morning and had to turn it around by that afternoon. The copy editors were all combing through it for misspelled words, misplaced commas, things like that. At this stage in the production schedule, called the "board stage," you can only make minor changes because the text is precisely spaced on the page. If for some reason you needed to take out a paragraph, for example, you would have to replace it with one of similar length, otherwise it would throw off the layout of each page and therefore throw off the pagination.

After lunch I was told by the rights and permissions department it would cost fifteen hundred dollars to use one of the quotes in the study guide. It was a beautiful quote, and I hated not to use it, but I knew the budget was tight, so I opted to replace it. But the quote was almost a page in length, and I couldn't find anything that would fit.

It was now a little more than two hours before the deadline. I strummed my fingers, looked at the clock. By five o'clock I had to have something on that page. The only way I could think to solve the spacing problem was to write a poem of my own. That way I could make it just the right length to replace the other one.

The subject of the study-guide lesson was Mary breaking an alabaster vial of perfume and anointing Jesus during the week when He was taken away to be crucified. So that is where I started, looking through a window at the home of Simon the Leper, where Mary and Martha, Lazarus, Jesus, and His disciples were all gathered.

Now the Passover and the Feast of Unleavened Bread were only two days away, and the chief priests and the teachers of the law were looking for some sly way to arrest Jesus and kill him. "But not during the Feast," they said, "or the people may riot."

While he was in Bethany, reclining at the table in the home of a man known as Simon the Leper, a woman came with an alabaster jar of very expensive perfume, made of pure nard. She broke the jar and poured the perfume on his head.

Some of those present were saying indignantly to one another, "Why this waste of perfume? It could have been sold for more than a year's wages and the money given to the poor." And they rebuked her harshly.

"Leave her alone," said Jesus. "Why are you bothering her? She has done a beautiful thing to me. The poor you will always have with you, and you can help them any time you want. But you will not always have me. She did what she could. She poured perfume on my body beforehand to prepare for my burial. I tell you the truth, wherever the gospel is preached throughout the world, what she has done will also be told, in memory of her" (Mark 14:1–9).

Some people have a romantic view of what the life of a writer is like. They think writers go out and sit by the sea with their notebook and pencil, muse awhile, write awhile, spread out the beach towel and tan awhile, muse awhile, write awhile, tear the ragged end off a loaf of French bread, smear it with a little Brie cheese, sip a little chardonnay, muse a while longer, write a while longer, and at the end of the day, savor what they've written like an after-dinner mint on a serene walk home.

The truth is, writing is mostly blue collar work, not much different from that of a stone mason. At least, it's that way for me. Every day I go to work where I pick through a rubble of words, looking for one that will fit, hoping the mortar will hold, that the work will stand up. I go back and forth from the word pile to the worksite all day long, looking for the right words and the right places to put them. And at the end of the day I dust myself off, wash up, and go home.

Hardly a day at the beach. Especially on a day like today with a five o'clock deadline heating up on the back of my neck like a sunburn. Instead of tearing off a piece of French bread, I was tearing off my fingernails an anxious bite at a time. I jotted notes on a legal pad, picked up a word here, a phrase there, discarded some of the things, set others aside.

As I worked, I found myself slipping into the story, sitting among the disciples as they watched Mary, catching their reaction in the corner of my eye, then turning to Jesus to catch His. What did Mary see about Him that day that the disciples didn't? What did He see about her that they didn't?

For a long time, nothing.

Then something deep inside seeped to the surface, rimming my eyes with sudden emotion.

And suddenly I have the right eyes.

Tearful eyes.

And through the blur of those tears, everything, paradoxically, became clear.

After two hours I finished typing the final draft, sent it down to our typesetter who spaced it on the page and sent it out to the printer, just in time. The following vignette is what I wrote.

Broken Vases

The aroma of extravagant love.
So pure. So lovely.
Flowing from the veined alabaster vase
*   of Mary's broken heart—*
A heart broken against the hard reality
*   of her Savior's imminent death.*
Mingled with tears, the perfume became—
*   by some mysterious chemistry of Heaven—*
Not diluted but more concentrated,
Potent enough behind the ears of each century
*   for the scent to linger to this day.*
Doubtless, the fragrance, absorbed by his garment,
*   as it flowed from his head,*
Accompanied Christ through the humiliation of his trials,
*   the indignity of his mockings,*

the pain of his beatings,
the inhumanity of his cross.
Through the heavy smell of sweat and blood,
A hint of that fragrance must have arisen
from his garment—
Until, at shameful last, the garment was stripped
and gambled away.
And maybe, just maybe, it was that scent
amid the stench of humanity rabbled around the cross,
that gave the Savior the strength to say:
"Father, forgive them, for they know not what they do."

And as Mary walked away from the cross,
The same scent probably still lingered in the now-limp hair
she used to dry the Savior's feet—
A reminder of the love that spilled
from his broken alabaster body.
So pure. So lovely.
So truly extravagant.
It was a vase he never regretted breaking.
Nor did she.

When I finished, I sat back and rested a moment in my chair. Then something remarkable happened. It was as if a fragrant whiff of Mary's love had come through the open window of that page and breezed through the stuffy rooms of my heart with such potency I could almost smell it.

Since I am a writer and since writing occupies so much of my time, I tend to sense God speaking more often in that area of my life than others, but maybe that's just because that's the area of my life where I am the most attentive. All I know is, He meets me there.

He also met the wise men there, where they worked. In the night skies with a sudden star. He met the shepherds there. In their fields as they

kept watch over their sheep. And He met me there too. In my office as I
watched over my words to meet a five o'clock deadline.

He met me there and brought me to a window in the Scriptures
and showed me an intimate moment that Mary had with the Savior. It was a
moment so pure and so lovely it brought tears to my eyes.

And something else.

It brought a project I would end up spending the next six years of
my life writing, a series of devotional books about the life of Christ that
began with *Intimate Moments with the Savior*.

Going from Texas to California, you have to pass through Death
Valley. Going from *A More Congenial Spot* to *Intimate Moments with the Savior*, I had to pass through a Death Valley of my own.

It's not the route I would have chosen. But it was the route God
used to take me from a more congenial spot in my relationship with Him to a
place that was a more intimate one.

And en route, He transformed the cologne of a formula romance
into the aroma of extravagant love.

A *Prayer for* Discovery

Help me, O God,

Help me to discover the gifts You have given me
and how to use those gifts in a way that is worthy of the giver.
Help me to discover something of who I am
from the things that I write,
whether those things are a letter or a journal entry
a poem or a play,
a novel or a note to friend.
In those lines and between those lines
help me discover how to live my life.
Grant that I might live it honestly,
without pretensions or pseudonyms,
and fragrantly,
with the aroma of extravagant love
spilling from the brokenness of my heart
onto Yours . . .

Windows of Scripture

You read books to borrow therefrom the force to stimulate your activity . . . but I read books searching for the man who has written them.

VINCENT VAN GOGH
in a letter to his youngest sister

There is a story about the famous illustrator and painter Gustave Doré in which one of his students had just finished a painting of Jesus and handed it to him for his critique. Doré studied it, his mind searching for the right words. At last he handed it back to the student.

"If you loved Him more," he said, "you would have painted Him better."

I knew I did not love Jesus enough to paint Him, let alone to paint Him well, certainly not well enough to do justice to the incomparable beauty of His life. Yet because of the window that opened that day at my office, letting in the fragrant aroma of Mary's love for Jesus, I felt compelled to try. At the same time, though, I felt too inadequate to even pick up a brush.

I felt like that little boy with the lunch basket among the five thousand grown men on that Galilean hillside, who for days had been listening to Jesus. You'd think Jesus would have picked one of the disciples to arrange for the food. He talked to Philip about it. And Andrew. But it wasn't either of them He picked. Or any of the other disciples.

It was a little boy.

Who even knew the boy's name? What did he even have to offer? Five small barley loaves. Two small fish. How far would that go among so many?

And as I was thinking about all the reasons why I shouldn't write a book about Christ, I suddenly realized. I was the little boy. It was my shoulder Jesus was tapping, my basket He was wanting.

He came to me not because of what I had to offer. He came to me because He wanted to show me what He could do with the coarsely ground loaves and the couple of slender fish that were my words. He wanted to show me how, if I gave them to Him, He could take them and bless them, multiply them and use them to nourish His people. The image of the little boy at the feeding of the five thousand helped put my feelings of inadequacy in perspective and helped me hand over the lunch basket.

Wondering where to start, I began looking over my shelves of theological books. It was there I made an unsettling discovery. I had more books on Greek grammar than I did on the life of Christ.

It was incriminating to realize that He who had given so much occupied so small a shelf in my life. In the quiet courtroom of my heart, I was suddenly the defendant, suddenly the one put on the witness stand and called to give an account of my life. The questions were indicting.

What had I been doing in seminary? Had I been learning how to live my life, or had I simply been learning how to use my gift?

What had I been pursuing those four years? A Savior, or simply a skill?

If the truth, the whole truth, and nothing but the truth were known, what verdict would be handed down to us, to you and to me, about what we've been pursuing for so much of our lives, and why?

Had I been reading the Bible the way van Gogh's sister read books, "to borrow therefrom the force to stimulate my activity?"

Had I read it, searching for principles, to make my life in some way more successful?

Had I read it, searching for promises, to make my life in some way more safe?

Had I read it, searching for proof texts, to give certainty to my own faith or make it more defensible to others?

Had I read it, searching for preaching material, because that was my job?

Had I read it, searching for power, for whatever reason?

Or had I read it, as van Gogh had read his books, searching for the man who wrote it?

Those thoughts came at a time when Judy and I were praying to hear God's voice, see His face, experience Him in our lives more deeply, more fully. Both of us had a personal relationship with Him, but we longed for more. We were both resting on a plateau in our spiritual lives, still weary from our time in the wilderness. And weary of each other. Both of us were thinking that if this was the best the view got, we weren't sure it was worth the climb. We weren't sure there was anything more to see, but we hoped there was.

It was a difficult time for us. Although we were in some respects out of the wilderness, we found that the boundary of the wilderness wasn't as neatly marked off as it had been for the Israelites. If we had crossed to the other side of the Jordan, we were still sloshing our way through its muddy banks. We were beginning to find that some of the sand from the wilderness had come with us. There were abrasions from the rub, and some of those spots were still tender. But at least we were going somewhere. We had come a long way together, over the years.

Judy has traveled with me through life when I was a student, a pastor, an oil-field equipment salesman, an unemployed writer, a wallpaper hanger, and a professional writer. She has left home and family and everything familiar to be my companion on this journey. She has gone from Fort Worth, Texas, to Nacogdoches to Poolville, then on to Fullerton, California, and from there to Monument, Colorado. And I have the confidence she will go with me to the ends of the earth.

We have been from better to worse and back again. And she's still with me. We have been richer and poorer, in more ways than merely financial. And she's still with me. We have been in sickness and in health, in more ways than merely physical. And she's still with me. Why? Because she loves me and has committed herself to me.

It is only natural for me to share with her the secrets of my heart, my innermost thoughts, my deepest longings, my hopes, my dreams, my plans for the future. The same is true in our relationship with Christ. In the Upper Room Jesus said to his disciples: "Whoever has my commands and obeys them, he is the one who loves me. He who loves me will be loved by my Father, and I too will love him and show myself to him."

In the context of a committed relationship, Jesus promises to show Hmself to us, reveal Himself, disclose to us the innermost secret of who He is. Often we want that intimate disclosure without being serious about the relationship. If you think about it, that's not much different from casual sex, wanting the pleasures of intimacy without the commitment. But Jesus is not indiscriminately intimate.

I spent a lot of time in seminary studying the Bible, and it led me to a lot of places. Hebrew. Greek. Systematic Theology. Hermeneutics. A lot of good places. And at those places I learned many of important things. But it was Mary, in an intimate moment with the Savior, who taught me what was most important. And it wasn't how pure my doctrine was. It was how passionate my devotion. That was what mattered to Jesus. That's what he defended. What He called beautiful. That's the picture He memorialized for all time.

Not everyone, though, shared his taste in art. The scribes and Pharisees, to name just a couple. They were the most biblically educated people in the world. They believed the right things. Taught the right things. Prided themselves in being scriptural. And yet . . .

And yet Jesus didn't prop any of their pictures on his mantel.

The pictures dear to Jesus, the ones He holds close to His heart, the ones that bring a tear to His eyes or a smile to His face are ones like Mary's. Because what touches His heart is not how much we know, but how much we love. Not how pure we are, but how passionate.

Maybe that is why, when Pharisees were fighting over theology, prostitutes were falling at the Savior's feet and slipping into the kingdom of God on their tears.

From that point on, my view of the Scriptures changed. I realized then that the Scriptures revealed a person who was searching for me, reaching out to me. A person who wanted not simply a personal relationship with me but an intimate one. Now when I read the Scriptures, I read searching.

I love my four children dearly. I am proud of them all and excited to show other people their pictures. I'm proud of how hard they work at school and what they bring home to show me, their artwork, spelling tests, reports they've written, books they've read. It's so wonderful watching them grow up, seeing them getting involved in life, doing things, learning things. But the most fulfilling thing I remember as their father is coming home when they were younger and hearing the first one who saw me, holler to the others,

"Dad's home!" And then to see them all come running, throwing their arms around me, showering me with hugs and kisses.

That was a long time ago. They're teenagers now. Their thoughts are other places when Dad comes home. Homework. Television. Household chores. Telephone. I was no different when I was their age.

We all grow up and grow out of our childlike enthusiasms. But maybe something of the little girl in Mary never did. And maybe one of the reasons she meant so much to the Savior was that she had a "Jesus is home!" type of excitement whenever she saw Him, and that sitting at His feet or anointing Him with perfume came as naturally as children throwing their arms around their daddy's legs and showering Him with hugs and kisses.

When the Lord wanted to brag about His children, He did so by showing us their pictures. Like a proud father, He takes out his wallet and says, "Do you want to see something beautiful, do you want to see what the delight of my life is, what I live for, what makes it all worth while? Here, take a look."

And He shows us a picture of Mary. Three of them, in fact. The first was one taken at Mary and Martha's home. The second was one at the death of their brother, Lazarus. The third was when she anointed Jesus with perfume.

As far as we know, Mary never prophesied, never preached a sermon, never wrote a book. In fact, of all the three pictures, in only one does she even speak. And then, only one sentence. She never worked a miracle, never healed anyone who was sick, never cast out a demon.

All she did was love the Savior.

It was the way she loved Him that made the difference. And it was the way Judy and I wanted to.

A window of the soul opened to Judy through a dream and to me through a deadline. For her, a girl in grubby-looking workout clothes and torn leggings led the way. For me, it was a boy with a meager-looking lunch basket. But both children were leading us to the same place—to a more intimate relationship with the Savior.

When I understood that, I realized Jesus had come to me that day in the office not because I loved Him so much, but because He wanted me to.

Because He wanted me to . . .

A *Prayer of* Intimacy

Help me, O God,

To treasure all the words in the Scriptures,
  but to treasure them only as they lead to You.
May the words be stepping-stones in finding You,
  and if I am to get lost at all in the search,
    may it not be down a theological rabbit trail,
      or in some briar patch of religious controversy.
If I am to get lost at all,
  grant that it be in Your arms.
Help me to love You the way Mary did.
And something of the spilling passion of her devotion, spill onto me.

Windows of Humanity

And the Word was made flesh, and dwelt among us, and we beheld his glory. . . .

JOHN 1:14

On a hill just above the freeway in the city where I grew up sat a large wholesale bakery, and everytime I drove past it, I would roll down my window and savor a deep breath. The smell of its freshly baked bread made my mouth water. It also made me remember how hungry I was, although maybe I had suppressed that hunger for most of the day.

Until I passed the bakery.

"I am the bread of life," said Jesus. "He who comes to me will never go hungry."

Sometimes when I hear those words, I can't help but think about that bakery by the freeway. And I can't help but think that if the bakery were open to the public, the traffic would be backed up for miles. That is what happened when the Bread of Heaven came down and offered Himself to the public. People came from miles around, lining up, hoping some small crust of something good might fall their way.

But Jesus returned to heaven, and for a while there was no bread. In His absence, though, he made sure the world would not go hungry.

He left the recipe for his life in the Scriptures. And He left His Spirit to blend its truths into our lives—flour and sugar, raw eggs and butter, everything. From there, the bare hands of circumstance were called in to knead the dough, a time of solitude was set aside to give the loaf a chance to rise, and the ovens of daily life were opened to bake it.

And once again, the aroma of freshly baked bread filled the earth.

The difference between the inscripturated word and the incarnate word is the difference between the recipe and the bread. As essential as the recipe is, it is not a recipe that attracts people most. It is not a billboard on the bakery. It is not a catchy ad campaign or colorful packaging or the promise of some prize inside.

It is the smell of freshly baked bread.

In smelling that bread, the soul instinctively salivates and is reminded of the hunger it has for so long been suppressing. It is the smell that entices the soul to taste, and the taste that entices it to eat. So often, though, instead of giving out bread to the hungry, we give out recipes.

The recipes come in all kinds of cookbooks. From Bibles to bumper stickers. From books to cassettes. From sermons to smidgens of advice. And all of them come full of words. Good words, many of them. Well-intentioned words, certainly. But words that have not been made flesh. Words that have not dwelt among us.

I wonder what would happen if one day all of those words went away. What if one day the entire body of Christ were struck dumb? Couldn't write a word. Couldn't speak a word. Couldn't even move our lips to mouth one. What then? What would be left?

Our lives.

And what would our lives say? What would they say about who we are and who our God is? What would they say about what we believe? If we were to take away the words, how much of the gospel could the world understand?

Would we discover that the world is illiterate? Or that our lives are illegible?

Would the writing on the pages of our lives, which we always took to be literature, turn out to be the scribbling of a preschooler? Or would the pages simply be blank?

"Preach the gospel," Saint Francis said, "and when necessary, use words." And he said that, I think, because he realized that the most impactful words are those incarnate in our lives. Words that have been made flesh and dwell among us.

When asked why he wanted to go to Africa to work among the natives, Albert Schweitzer said it was because he wanted his life to be his sermon. He wanted the days of his week to be a Sunday text so clear and so compelling that little else needed to be said. As it turned out, little else needed be. His life was heard by millions.

There is a story of another missionary whose life was not heard by millions. He was an English missionary in India whose mission board required him to keep detailed financial records for which he had to be skilled at double-entry bookkeeping. Which he wasn't. He had no background in accounting or business. He only had a calling. To be a missionary. But his balances were always off, and the separate accounts he was supposed to keep kept getting mixed, and so the mission board released him. Unfit for the mission field, was their assessment, when in truth, he was only unfit for bookkeeping. He left without incident. Nobody knew where.

Years later, a woman missionary visited a remote jungle village to introduce the natives to Jesus. She told them of His kindness and His love for the poor, how He went to their homes to eat with them, how He visited them when they were sick, how He fed the hungry, healed the sick, bound up the wounds of the brokenhearted, and how children loved to follow Him.

The eyes of the natives lit up, their faces beamed, and one of them exclaimed: "Miss Sahib, we know him well; he has been living here for years!"

When they took her to see him, it was the man who years earlier had been dismissed by the mission board. He had settled there to do his work, sequestered from the double-entried tyranny of bookkeeping. Whenever anyone was sick, he visited them and waited up all night outside their hut if necessary, checking on them, tending to their needs. When they were hurt, he nursed their wounds. For the old and the infirm, he brought food and water. When cholera broke out in the village, he went from hut to hut, doing what he could to help.

I wonder. If someone were to come to our village, our neighborhood, our place of work, and that person began to describe Jesus, would anybody hearing the description say, "We know Him well; He has been living here for years!"

The downtown bakery was eventually torn down, and a new one built on the outskirts. A bigger one, more modern, more efficient. It was one of the places, coincidentally, that I had applied for work when I was an unemployed writer. One of the many other places happened to be in California. I traveled there, looking for work, trying to sell the screen rights to a book I wrote, but after a week of knocking on doors I was ready to come home.

It was there I was shown a window of the soul.

I was staying at a friend's house in Los Angeles at the time, and my last day there I took a walk to unwind. I took with me a notebook and pen, and after walking awhile, I stopped to chronicle the week. As I was writing, a homeless woman edged into my peripheral vision. I looked up. She was making slow progress down the sidewalk on the other side of the street in front of an elementary school, its playground a burst seedpod of children.

The picture was so poignant, her standing there, barely able to walk; the children on the other side of the fence, running everywhere, laughing, calling to one another, chasing one another, *tag-you're-it.* I turned to a clean page and tried to capture what I could of what I saw, titling it "Without Bootstraps."

Without Bootstraps

At Rosewood and Croft,
Where the parochial school sits as a hive of morning activity,
The solitary eye at the intersection, blinking amber,
Looks down the gray hem of street
Where a dull needle of a woman
Stitches her way inconspicuously
Through the seams in the sidewalk.

A snarl of lusterless hair
Is held captive by the wooled frizz of a dingy ski cap.
Skin tessellated with age,
The slack leather baggage of too many travels jowls her face.

A patchwork of Salvation Army polyester stretches and sags
Over this tattered quilt of a woman.
Her bulky, open sweater hangs incongruous to the day,
While the timid, dirty face of a wrinkled hanky
Peeks marsupially from her pocket.

A tired woman, the weight of sixty-some years
Carried on her dowager's hump,
Slumping her at an angle tangent to the sidewalk,
She plods along, a camel too long in the desert.

Pushing shackles of lead, ill-fitting faded Converse All-Stars,
She shuffles her rubber soles over the concrete,
As if bulky gum erasers in hands too small,
Clumsily attempting to erase a schoolgirl's mistakes.

Her two-wheeled shopping caddie follows like a stray,
A vestigial shininess clinging to it, almost stubbornly,
And holds prisoner a frayed, shriveled clump of garbage bags.

The amber eye looks past her, blinking,
As the bent needle of a woman threads her way along the gray hem of street,
Motif'd in brocades of Los Angeles plumage.

All around her is green,
But she sees only gray,
Her life, no longer marked off by birthdays,
But by measured seams in the sidewalk.
And somewhere inside is a little girl,
Forever fenced from the playgrounds.

I looked. I listened. And I framed her life with my words. The picture, with the elementary school serving as a backdrop, revealed something I might not have seen if recess had been ten minutes earlier or later. The woman was not always who she was now, wasn't always like she was now, or where she was now. And the playground teeming with children brought that into sharp relief.

She was a little girl once. A little girl who went to school and looked forward to recess. Certainly she skipped rope. Flamingoed her way through hopscotch. Played ring-around-the-rosie. Maybe she giggled with her friends over a schoolgirl crush. Looked forward to birthdays and sparkly fireworks on the Fourth of July. Maybe she had a pet of some kind, a puppy, a kitty cat, something she cared for and that cared for her. I hope she did. Certainly she hung out an empty stocking on Christmas Eve. Couldn't get to sleep for all the excitement tingling inside her. And dreamed through her dolls and dress-up clothes what her life might someday be.

But her someday has become a sidewalk and a shopping cart. And there are no dolls to go back to, or dreams to look forward to.

The sight of that woman hobbling down that sidewalk in front of that playground was a window of the soul. It showed me something of the sadness of those whose life is the street. Something of the sidewalk monotony of their lives. And the meandering tragedy of a soul slowly walking itself to death. The picture of that woman on the street was a window of the soul, and I received at least something of what it had to offer.

But what had I given in return?

There is more to windows of the soul than what we receive there. Something is also required. Sometimes it is a very small thing. Sometimes it is our very life. What is it God expects from us at those intersecting moments like the one at Rosewood and Croft?

Is not this what I require of you as a fast:
to loose the fetters of injustice,
to untie the knots of the yoke,
to snap every yoke?
and set free those who have been crushed?
Is it not sharing your food with the hungry,
taking the homeless poor into your house,
clothing the naked when you meet them
and never evading a duty to your kinfolk?
(Isaiah 58:6–7 NEB)

It is how the Word of God dwelt among us. And how He dwells among us still. Except now, it is our flesh He slips into. What else could it mean to be called the body of Christ, if it is not His feet we are becoming,

His hands? If it is not going where His feet went and doing what His hands did, what is it?

> Whose eyes will brim with compassion for the multitudes, if not ours?
> Whose arms will embrace the prodigals, if not ours?
> Whose hands will touch the lepers, if not ours?

Other than the palette of emotions I had for the homeless woman at Rosewood and Croft, and the few brushstrokes of prayer I made on her behalf, my life did not affect that picture. I observed it, but I did not enter into it, wasn't a part of its color or composition. But this is the whole point of windows of the soul. Always looking. Always listening. Always asking at those windows: What is here that I should receive? What is required of me at this moment? And how will I respond?

The following is a picture I was a part of, if only for an evening.

Judy and I were driving on the freeway in Fort Worth in the drenching rain when we came across a stalled car on the shoulder of the road where two women were standing in the downpour. We stopped, picked them up, and took the off-ramp to the nearest phone booth. As we pulled up to one, our headlights revealed a man beating a woman. I jumped out of the car to break it up, and the man told me it was his "old lady," as if that somehow sanctioned the abuse. I stepped between them and broke up the fight, and he stood with clenched fists and asked if I wanted to fight. Before I could answer, the woman fell to the ground and hit her head on the concrete. We both bent down to help her. Her head was bleeding and her eyes rolled back in her head. I told him I thought she might be pretty badly hurt and that we needed to call an ambulance. He told me then that he had been in jail and couldn't "stick around." And in an incongruous moment of tenderness, he touched my hand, which was holding his "old lady," and gently squeezed it. "Thanks," he said, and ran off.

Within a few minutes the ambulance and police came. The woman was high on something but, as it turned out, not badly hurt. She refused to go to the hospital and lied to the police about her name. She told them it was Kathy. It was actually Denise, unless of course she had lied to me. When the police questioned her, she refused to file charges against the man who beat her. Another incongruous moment. An act of protection, maybe. Maybe even an act of love.

Since the police wouldn't take her and the ambulance wouldn't take her, we took her. She was twenty-three, we found out, had gotten pregnant at thirteen and given the baby up for adoption, had been living with the man who beat her for the past three-and-a-half years. His name was Buckwheat, she told us. She had no friends and only twenty-six cents to her name.

We took her to Judy's mother's house, where her mother washed her hair and cleaned the cut on her head, served her some chicken noodle soup along with some Ritz crackers and a cup of coffee. We cleaned her up, dried her off, fed her, gave her our address and the address of a nearby church, and tried as best we could to provide a little shelter from the stormy life she had. After a few hours, she asked us to take her to a convenience store on West Berry, near where she lived. She was afraid if she was gone too long the man who beat her would beat her again. We talked to her about going to a shelter for battered women, but it would just cause more trouble, she told us. And so we dropped her off, sadly, knowing that though we had dried her off, we were sending her back into the storm.

At the time, I didn't ask the picture what it required of me. It all happened so fast. I didn't have time to think, just to react. It was clear what was required of me, to step between the man who was beating the woman. I entered the picture of this battered woman's life with what amounted to only a few touches of human kindness. Nothing more. It was help, but only for an evening. Nothing more. Although there is a little more. I still think of Denise and Buckwheat now and then, and whenever I do, I dab a little prayer into the paint, hoping it might somehow change the picture. And if indeed more things *are* wrought by prayer than this world dreams of, who knows what may happen? Maybe nothing. Maybe everything.

My point in telling you these stories is that the very least we should do is look. If we turn our head away, our heart will go with it. But if we look, maybe what we see there will in some way draw us into the picture. If we look with the right eyes, what we see will cause us to dig into the pockets of our humanity for something more than a little loose change. A sympathetic feeling, maybe. Or a heartfelt prayer. A kind word. A gentle touch. An understanding smile. Perhaps a listening ear. A hot meal, if only for a day. A shelter from the storm, if only for an evening.

And why?

Why should we stop? Why should we look? Why should we enter the picture?

Because it is what Jesus did. And what He would do if He were here. It is to those people He came. And to those people He wants to come again. But He is in heaven. And if He is to come to them at all, it must be through us.

At these windows of the soul, something is required of us. It is for us to listen and find out what that something is. And it is for us to respond with our lives. We can't do everything. But we can do something. And if it is done in His name, even if it's a very little thing, it is something beautiful.

The Vatican City houses some of the most beautiful works of art in the history of humanity. The ceiling of the Sistine Chapel. The white marble sculpture of David. Saint Peter's Cathedral. The Pietà. But these are not the Church's great art.

These are:

"I tell you the truth," said Jesus of the widow's offering at the temple, "this poor widow has put more into the treasury than all the others. They all gave out of their wealth; but she, out of her poverty, put in everything— all she had to live on."

"Only one thing is needed," said Jesus to Martha, regarding her sister's quiet act of devotion of sitting at His feet. "Mary has chosen what is better, and it will not be taken away from her."

"She has done a beautiful thing to me," commented Jesus on Mary anointing Him with perfume, and "wherever the gospel is preached throughout the world, what she has done will also be told, in memory of her."

"Then the King will say to those on his right, 'Come, you who are blessed by my Father; take your inheritance, the kingdom prepared for you since the creation of the world. For I was hungry and you gave me something to eat, I was thirsty and you gave me something to drink, I was a stranger and you invited me in, I needed clothes and you clothed me, I was sick and you looked after me, I was in prison and you came to visit me. . . . I tell you the truth, whatever you did for one of the least of these brothers of mine, you did for me.'"

The great art of the church is not the words we put on paper or the paint we put on canvas. What words of grace we say, what acts of justice we do, what little kindnesses we show along the way, and the quiet, unpretentious ways we go about loving God and loving people, these are the Last Suppers and the Sistine Chapels and the Pietàs.

"The more I think it over," said van Gogh, "the more I feel that there is nothing more truly artistic than to love people."

The more I think it over, so do I.

A Prayer for Incarnation

Help me, O God,

To live the recipe
before I give the recipe.
Give me the kneading strength
to work the words into the doughy recesses of my life.
Help me to leave it alone a while
so it can rise.
Help me not to fear the oven
so it can bake.
And grant that in the baking,
the world would be able to roll down its window
and savor the aroma of freshly baked bread . . .

Windows of Tears

Whenever you find tears in your eyes, especially unexpected tears, it is well to pay the closest attention.

They are not only telling you something about the secret of who you are, but more often than not God is speaking to you through them of the mystery of where you have come from and is summoning you to where, if your soul is to be saved, you should go next.

FREDERICK BUECHNER
Whistling in the Dark

Perhaps there are no greater windows of the soul than our tears. The tears we cry are drawn from the well of who we are, a well that lies beneath the sedimentary strata of words, beneath even the Precambrian layer of consciousness itself. They may seep to the surface like the smallest of subterranean springs or shoot to the surface like a geyser. They surface for odd reasons, or for no reason at all, or for reasons so pure and right and good that no force on earth could hold them back.

I think of the tears I have cried over the years, and by pooling them into one place, I can see rippling in it a reflection of myself. I'm not talking about the kinds of tears that come with a skinned knee from falling off your childhood bike. I'm talking about tears that come from a different place than that, a place you can't put your finger on but somehow manages to put one on you.

I'm thinking about some of those places in my own life. One of them was the first time I remember seeing my father cry. He used to be a football coach and one day received news that one of his former players had been killed in a car accident, and at the funeral we passed the open casket, where he suddenly broke down sobbing. I was on the cusp of growing up, twelve, maybe thirteen, and I wasn't sure how people were supposed to act at funerals, but seeing my father in such sudden pain, weeping such hard tears, I couldn't help from sobbing too.

Tears also came September 12, 1986, at 4:36 in the morning when the phone rang in the dark and I heard the words, "Dad died."

Górecki's *Third Symphony* almost always brings tears, but I don't know why. Judy Garland singing "Somewhere Over the Rainbow" at the beginning of *The Wizard of Oz*, and her repeating "There's no place like home" at the end. One or the other usually brings tears. Sometimes both.

"The Bible was written in tears," said A. W. Tozer, "and to tears it yields its best treasures." Some of those treasures came to me that way when I was working on the *Moments with the Savior* series.

At a Young Life camp, tears came when I was a college counselor to a cabin of inner-city kids. Unthinkingly I had alienated them, and what brought tears was not the thought that they were alienated from me but the thought that because of me they might be alienated from Christ, maybe forever.

At some time or another I have cried for each of my children at different times in their lives and for different reasons. I've wept when I've been harsh with them and had time to think about how that harshness might be understood by someone who was just a child.

Tears came when I visited Camarillo State Hospital to see a mentally handicapped friend staying there. Seeing all that bent and broken humanity collected in one place, hidden away from everybody's eyes, broke my heart. But it was when I was standing outside the hospital, wishing with all my heart that Jesus could just stop by with all His mending and straightening power and make everything right, and knowing that it was just me stopping by and that stopping by was the best I could do ... that is what made me cry.

The prayer sung by Jean Valjean in the stage play *Les Miserables*, pleading for God's protection of a young man going off to battle, spoke to me with the fluid eloquence of tears. And maybe it did because I have a son, who, though he is too young to go off to war, won't always be, and already within me I feel Valjean's prayer moving to its knees.

I cry when the von Trapp family sings "Edelweiss" in the movie *The Sound of Music*, especially the part where Christopher Plummer can't go on singing and Julie Andrews picks up where he left off, giving him, the whole family, the whole audience, the courage to sing.

When the coach's old gray car drove across the screen at the beginning of the movie *Hoosiers*, I wept. My dad had a car like that when he drove into the small town of McKinney, Texas, to take his first coaching job, and for a moment it brought him back to me.

I cried as I prayed for the shell of a man in the final stages of cancer, knowing he was a young man with still half his life ahead of him, and knowing he was leaving behind a young wife and three boys, knowing all of them would be living all of their lives without him, and wishing so desperately it was Jesus at his bedside instead of me.

My eyes moisten sometimes when I wake up before Judy does, and I see her lying there, and I realize what a joy she is to me, what wonderful memories we have shared, the laughter, the love. And lying there, watching her, I realize that someday I will wake up and she will not be on the other side of my bed, or that she will wake up and I will not be on the other side of hers. And the thought of that is too sad and too lonely to bear without the company of tears.

Each of those tearful moments is a window. In each of those windows is something that not only sanctifies the moment but transcends the moment. In each tear is distilled something of eternity, something of love and compassion and tenderness, all things that originate in heaven and come to earth as a sacrament to my soul, if only I am willing to take and to eat.

The closest communion with God comes, I believe, through the sacrament of tears. Just as grapes are crushed to make wine and grain to make bread, so the elements of this sacrament come from the crushing experiences of life.

And sometimes the crushing starts early.

One day your dog doesn't come home, and you go calling for it. Another day passes, and you go looking for it. And on the third day when you're looking for it, you find its stiff body on the side of a well-trafficked street, and you bundle it up, carry it off, dig a hole in the backyard, and you bury it with a rock as a tombstone and tears as a eulogy.

Or someone at school dies from a cerebral hemorrhage or several someones, in a sudden car wreck.

Or someone you've fallen in love with hasn't fallen in love with you, and you think life can't go on.

Or you learn from the orthopedic doctor that you can no longer play the sport you have loved for half of your still very young life, and maybe it's not the thing that should bring tears, but it does.

Or a grandparent dies. A grandparent who loved you and teased you and hugged you and brought "a little something for you" every time she came to visit. And now there's a freshly dug hole in the backyard of your heart.

Or a parent dies, and now the whole backyard is one big hole.

Or a marriage ends between two people you thought would be the last to break up, and besides the grief you feel, you sense the mortar of life loosening a little, and the unsettling feeling that if it could happen to them, it could happen to anyone, even to you.

Like the dark woods of a fairy tale, life too has its dark side. And somewhere down the road, if we travel long enough down that road, we will experience it. Who knows what woods that road will take us through or what frightening things may be crouching in their shadows?

In Dante's *Inferno,* the writer is taking a walk and suddenly finds himself disoriented, and so begins his journey into the various levels of hell with these words:

> *In the middle of the journey of our life*
> *I found myself in a dark wood.*

In the middle of my own journey I found myself in such a wood. But it is only partially my story and I would rather not tell any of it than risk telling the part of it that is not mine to tell. What I can say is this: The darkness of the woods was more terrifying than the starkness of the wilderness.

It was for me a time of depression in which the trees were so dense and their shadows so long that I didn't know how to get out—or if I ever would get out. That was the fear. Not the darkness of the woods. Not the dangers in the shadows. But that the woods may never end.

I feared too for someone I loved whose life had also ended up in the woods, only in a different one from mine, lost too but in a different way. I wanted with all my heart to help but found myself of all people the least capable of doing it.

And so the sun went down and the woods got dark, and with the darkness came the tears. There I was, huddled in the rain, shivering, and the only thing I could do was pray for the dawn.

So much is distilled in our tears, not the least of which is wisdom in living life. From my own tears I have learned that if you follow your tears, you will find your heart. If you find your heart, you will find what is dear to God. And if you find what is dear to God, you will find the answer to how you should live your life.

A Prayer for Courage

Help me, O God.

Give me the courage to cry.
Help me to understand that tears bring
freshly washed colors arching across the soul,
colors that wouldn't be there apart from the rain.
Help me to see in the prism of my tears,
something of the secret of who I am.
Give me the courage
not only to see what those tears are revealing
but to follow where they are leading.
And help me to see,
somewhere over the rainbow,
that where they are leading me is home . . .

Windows of Depression

I think I shall always remember this black period with a kind of joy, with a pride and faith and deep affection that I could not at the time have believed possible, for it was during this time that somehow I survived defeat and lived my life through to a first completion, and through the struggle, suffering, and labor of my own life came to share some of those qualities in the lives of people all around me.

THOMAS WOLFE
The Autobiography of an American Novelist

In *Letters to a Young Poet,* the older poet Rilke advised that it was "important to be lonely and attentive when one is sad."

I called out desperately to hear God during my long night in the woods. I called for direction, for understanding, for help. I asked for a way out, and if not a way out, at least a footprint letting me know He was somewhere in the woods with me, a broken twig, something, anything. Had I been calling out too long or too loudly to hear His answer? I had certainly been lonely enough in my depression, but had I been attentive enough?

It was a day that lent itself to being attentive when I finally did hear something, or thought I did. It was a spring day. The day before, the temperature reached a high of eighty-three degrees. Today, though, there was six inches of snow. I walked in the backyard, stood, looked, listened.

A gesture of wind touched my face. The sound of a dog barking, sounding faraway but wasn't. The sound of faraway birds that weren't. The snow muffled everything, making everything seem distant, seeming as if the world had stepped back to give you room, to give you a space of your own where thoughts of your own could stretch and move around.

I looked around, slowly, not wanting to force anything or manipulate the moment in any way. And I saw plants pushing their way through the snow, struggling to be green, or so it seemed as I watched them. Two seasons were competing for the same ground. Spring struggling to be born. Winter struggling not to die. And it seemed to me some sort of parable. Was it a parable for me?

Then the husk of the parable opened up, revealing a kernel of truth. Something inside me was struggling to be born. Something else was struggling not to die. And they were both inside me at the same time, winter and spring, contesting each other. The ending of one was necessary for the beginning of the other. A *new* beginning. I sensed it, sensed a seasonal shift within me. A stirring of the soil. A feeling that some germinating seed was unfurling itself.

Within a week the snow had melted, and spring seemed to have won the contest. I was in the backyard again, looking over the sloping part of the yard I had mowed last fall, noticing how green it was in contrast to all the brown stubble bordering it that had not been mowed. I began raking the pine needles that had quietly over the years woven a thatch carpet under the trees, hoping to see what plants were beneath. But beneath it the ground was bare as a hardwood floor. So I decided to water the ground to see what might come up, and if nothing did, I would seed it with wildflowers. I continued clearing the area, taking a shovel and evicting a squatter's camp of skunk cabbage, and after working up a sweat, I sat down and rested against one of the pines.

I sat there, trying to be attentive, wondering what clue God might be offering to help me solve the mystery of what my life had become. And suddenly, effortlessly, a clue seemed to come.

If new growth were to come to the backyard, the stubble must be mowed, the pine needles raked, the skunk cabbage dug up. What is now green and new was brought forth by the whirling blade of the lawnmower, the metal teeth of the rake, and the sharp edge of the shovel. The ground needed to be cleared before new growth could appear.

The plunge of the shovel. The drag of the rake. The spin of the blade. What if the ground were sentient, I wondered? If the stubble and the ground and the plants in it could all feel, what would that feel like? Like I felt all year. It was all very much like cutting and clearing and digging. If new life were indeed sprouting within me, it must have space to grow.

Depression is a burying of the soul in the ground, where it waits in the cold, lonely darkness, silent, solitary, waiting for the coming of spring, the warmth of the sun, and the companionship of all living things. "Except a grain of wheat fall to the ground and die, it cannot bear fruit." Depression, I learned, is not only the dark soil into which the grain falls but also the soil out of which grows the fruit.

But what fruit had grown out of that soil?

A sense of my tentative place in the universe, I think. The mortality not only of my life but of my livelihood. The mortality of my moods too, that is what I realized. That it is all a gift. Life. The people you love and who love you. Your health. The job you have, the skill you have to do it, even the strength to do it. Each and every one of those things is a gift. Understanding that it is a gift makes you treasure the gift all the more, enjoy it all the more, and live life not only with a greater sense of appreciation but of indebtedness.

Another fruit that came was the bittersweet knowledge of how little control I had over life, even my very own life, how little control any of us have over the storms that come into our lives or into the lives of those we love. Sometimes all you can do is to hold on for dear life until the storm passes.

There is an empathy for others that grew from all this, an understanding I didn't have before, a compassion. And the tears allowed me to touch the hem of Christ's sorrows. It was a very small hem and a very brief touch, but it gave me a greater understanding of the sadness He carried with Him as he walked this earth. And with that understanding came a deeper love.

The road Christ walked while He was here was a road that led to a tomb. I forget that sometimes. But out of that tomb came new life. Sometimes I forget that too.

It was a difficult road for Him to walk and a difficult one for us to follow, and who knows what terrifying things we may encounter along the way? Or what beautiful things may emerge down the road?

"If only we arrange our life," said Rilke, "according to that principle which counsels us that we must always hold to the difficult, then that which now still seems to us the most alien will become what we most trust and find most faithful. How should we be able to forget those ancient myths that are at the beginning of all peoples, the myths about dragons that at the last moment turn into princesses; perhaps all the dragons in our lives are princesses who are only waiting to see us once beautiful and brave. Perhaps everything terrible is in its deepest being something helpless that wants help from us."

Holding to the difficult was not easy. But in the end, it was the difficult that proved most faithful to my soul. And I found that dragons sometimes really do turn into princesses.

In closing his letter to an aspiring young poet, Rilke said: "Do not believe that he who seeks to comfort you lives untroubled among the simple and quiet words that sometimes do you good. His life has much difficulty and sadness and remains far behind yours. Were it otherwise he would never have been able to find those words."

Were it otherwise, maybe I would never have been able to find them either.

And maybe that too was some of the fruit.

"The sun'll come out, tomorrow," sang Orphan Annie with belting optimism.

But for me it didn't.

Six months I waited. Nine. A year. But no sun. A year and a half and still no sun. During that long, dark night I went to my office and tried to write, but it all seemed so pointless. I tried reading but couldn't concentrate. Some days I would come and just sit there, staring out the window. And after putting in a good day of sitting, I would go home.

I prayed, but I ended up on the floor, crying myself to sleep.

I wrote, or tried to. I had a project that was due, but the deadline came and went. Went and kept on going. I couldn't write a decent paragraph, let alone a decent page. A sentence. I could write a sentence, several sentences even. I just couldn't string them together in a way that made sense.

After months of this, I came home one day with a diagnosis.

"Judy, I think I'm depressed."

I'll never forget her response.

"Ken, you've been depressed for the last twelve years."

Not exactly the Orphan Annie song I was hoping for. But even if it wasn't what I wanted to hear, it was what I needed to. Hearing it, though, made me even more depressed. And more introspective. I'm slow at getting things sometimes but . . . *twelve years!*

Knock, knock. Anybody home? HELLO. Anybody in there?

I went to a doctor to find out. Fortunately, both of us were in. And between the medication and the exercise, the love of a wife and the prayers of friends, a good counselor and the person I love coming out of the woods too, the sun finally came out. Annie was right.

She just had lousy timing.

A Prayer for the Dawn

Dear God,

Someone once said:
  "Learning to weep, learning to keep vigil, learning to wait for the dawn.
   Perhaps this is what it means to be human."
Thank You for whoever said it,
  and teach me, I pray, how to live it.
Teach me how to weep
  without drowning in self-pity.
Teach me how to keep vigil
  even when I'm shivering in the dark.
And teach me how to wait for the dawn
  without the belting optimism of someone
    who hasn't been through the night . . .

Windows of Nature

A river, though, has so many things to say that it is hard to know what it says to each of us.

Norman Maclean
A River Runs Through It

A mother's love is translated through the breast she offers her newborn, through the gently rocked cradle of her arms, through the tenderness of her smile and the lullaby inflections of her voice. Although the baby cannot understand the depths of its mother's love, it can understand the softness of her breast, the warmth of her milk, and the gentleness of her voice.

Nature was such a mother to me, growing up. I was suckled in its leafy arms, rocked by the gentle rhythms of its rivers, calmed by the voices of its mourning doves cooing in the gray margins of the day. Although I didn't understand all I received there, what I received nourished me and became part of me and helped me grow in ways I am only now beginning to understand.

Much of what I received came from the Trinity River. It was almost lunar in its influence on me, pulling at the tides of my spirit, ebbing, flowing, taking me there in the morning, bringing me back late in the day, especially summer days.

I went to the river to see what it had to offer. Sometimes it was sunfish. Sometimes it was crawdads or tadpoles or minnows. Every once in a while, a turtle.

The first thing you did when you got there was to note all the tracks that crisscrossed the banks. Cryptic as cuneiform, the paw prints on the clay banks had written stories, and if you studied them, you could learn what went on the night before. After that, you baited your hook and cast your line and see what the river had to offer.

You can see the hook a few feet below the bobber. One by one the smaller sunfish are getting up the courage to charge the bait, which today is raw bacon, because bacon looks more like something a fish would eat than anything else that was in this morning's refrigerator.

The bigger fish, meanwhile, are watching, an aloof distance away. Food critics. You're hoping for one of *them*. What the river offers you, though, is a sunfish so small you wonder how it could have opened its mouth that wide to take the bait. It's not much, but as a boy on the banks, you take what you can get.

You take something else too, though you don't know it at the time. You see a water snake S-ing its way below the surface. Or a crawdad the size of lobster. Or a dead alligator gar in two feet of water, and it's as big as you are, looking like some extinct, prehistoric sea creature. That something else you take from the river is a sense of wonder at the murky mystery of it all. That is what brings you back as a kid.

And that is what brought me back as an adult.

We were planning to move from southern California but weren't sure where. Judy and I discussed a few places, finally narrowing them to Texas and Colorado. What helped us decide between the two, at least helped me, was the movie *A River Runs Through It*.

When I saw it, something eddied around the ankles of my soul, aswirl with memories of all those days on the Trinity River and those especially magical days in the Canadian wilderness where, as a Boy Scout, I had taken a 120-mile canoe trip. I realized none of my kids had experienced much of those things, but that it wasn't too late for them. That, as much as anything, is why we ended up in Colorado.

"The heavens declare the glory of God," says the psalm, day after sunlit day, night after starlit night. There are few places you can hear that declaration spoken so articulately as in parts of Colorado.

That God speaks through Nature is something taught not only in the Scriptures but in seminaries. In seminary you are taught Hebrew, the language of the Old Testament, and Greek, the language of the New. In some seminaries you can even take Aramaic, a cognate language in which a very small portion of the Bible was written, a few chapters in Daniel, a couple in Ezra, a verse in Jeremiah. Nature, it seems to me, is every bit as cryptic as the Hebrew script used in the Old Testament, and it seems a gap in the curriculum that there are courses teaching us how to translate the manuscripts of the Bible but none teaching us how to translate what naturalist John Muir referred to as "the manuscripts of God."

We are taught how to parse verbs but not the seasons, how to do word studies but not how to trace the etymologies in Nature back to their origin. We draw truths to live by from Solomon's Proverbs but not from

Nature's. We study the Davidic Psalms but not the divine ones in Nature, which chorus praise as well as cry out lament, and which groan along with David for its rescue and redemption.

If one and the same hand penned them both, are not both in some way speaking to us?

"All nature seems to speak," said van Gogh. "As for me, I cannot understand why everybody does not see it or feel it; nature or God does it for everyone who has eyes and ears and a heart to understand."

In our search for God, Nature is one of the places we look and one of the places He looks for us, reaches to us, speaks to us. If, indeed, Nature is one of the cognate languages of God, it seems only logical it would be one of the languages we should study.

Solomon was such a student. Jewish historian Josephus tells us that he "spake a parable upon every sort of tree, from the hyssop to the cedar; and in like manner also about beasts, about all sorts of living creatures, whether upon the earth, or in the seas, or in the air; for he was not unacquainted with any of their natures, nor omitted inquiries about them, but described them like a philosopher."

"Go to the ant, you sluggard; consider its ways and be wise!" says Solomon.

Where did Solomon get his eyes and his ears and his heart to understand?

God appeared to him in a dream at Gibeon, telling him to ask for whatever he wanted. When he asked for "a discerning heart" so he could have the wisdom to rule God's people, it pleased God so much He granted the request beyond Solomon's wildest dreams.

It's interesting to note that the word *discerning* comes from the Hebrew word that means "to hear." A "hearing heart" is what Solomon literally asked for, a heart that could look at an overgrown field or an ant at work and see windows of the soul. That same word is used in the great commandment, "*Hear*, O Israel: The Lord our God, the Lord is one. Love the Lord your God with all your heart and with all your soul and with all your strength." The first step toward being wise is also the first step in loving God, and that is being attentive to the words He has spoken.

When I moved to Colorado, I tried doing that, especially being attentive to what God might be saying through Nature.

I think I might have heard something the day I went down to put a penny on the railroad tracks. Something I always wanted to do as a kid, but I never lived close to a railroad. Now, the Sante Fe Railroad clacks by my office several times a day. And today I go to the tracks to pick up a small joy unclaimed from my childhood.

I put a line of pennies on the polished rail and returned later to find them all thin as aspen leaves. I palmed them all the way back to my office, looking at them with such childlike delight I almost stepped in a mud puddle. It was a shallow puddle and murky, and yet I could still see the sun reflected in it. Even in its muddy perimeter there was a glistening of sun.

I guess it was seeing the sun in the puddle while holding the flattened pennies in my hand that I realized something. No matter how defaced the coin, I could still tell it was a penny. I could tell by the copper color and the round shape and by the faint outline of Lincoln's face that somehow survived the train. And even though the puddle was shallow and muddy, I could still see the sun. Even in the mud I could see a glistening of it.

Even in Buckwheat beating up his "old lady" there was something beneath the brutality. One moment his hands were balled into fists, ready to fight. The next they were gently touching my hand, and after explaining why he couldn't stay, he said "Thank you" before running off. Even in the rain and in the muddy mess Buckwheat's life had become, something of the sun still glistened. Even in the loose change of his actions, I could still see traces of God's image on the coin.

Another day I took a walk up the mountains behind my office, and I sat on the banks of the Palmer Lake Reservoir, which was just beginning to thaw. The entire lake was covered with ice, except for the six-inch margin closest to shore. I was looking in the clear water to the pebbles a few inches below the surface when I caught a reflection of the sun in its rippling surface.

The light was broken into a prism of colors, and behind the prism was a veil of clouds, and behind the clouds the sun. I looked up to see this beautiful image in the sky, but even through the clouds, even through the filter of the earth's atmosphere, even through a distance of ninety-three million miles, my eyes couldn't take in the sun without having to shield them with my hand. I could only take it in looking at the reflection in that six-inch margin of water, and then, only when veiled by the clouds and rippled by the wind.

We cannot look at the sun in its noonday glory; only in the early mornings or late afternoons when it is filtered through the dust on the horizon, mirrored off the ripples of a pond, reflected off the face of the moon or the faces of the rest of creation that borrow its light.

Neither can we see God in His glory. It must be veiled or it would blind us. And so He comes to us in ways that our senses can take Him in without injury, which is always less than He is. And this helped me understand why God speaks to us in the ways He sometimes does.

Another day after a walk, I scrabbled up an ermined shoulder of mountain, found a dry spot, and sat among the pines. It was a day when I had no monologue of words to offer, no To-Do List to give God, no grocery list of requests. I wanted, in fact, not to pray, not to say anything. Just to sit and be quiet, that's all. And to listen.

Were there any gifts God had to offer me through the forest, through *this* forest? Anything in *this place* in the forest, *this day* in the forest, that might be for me, might in some way offer me direction at this juncture in my spiritual journey?

The person I loved but couldn't seem to communicate with was still very much in my thoughts, my prayers, my heart. But I didn't know how to respond, what I should say or do, or if even I should say or do anything. There was a specific, unresolved conflict that I didn't know how to handle. I had gotten advice from others, but the advice was conflicting, and I still was confused. Should I be firm and unyielding, make the person pay the consequences? Or should I be forgiving and pay them myself?

I sat there for a long time, knees scrunched to my chest, lost in the folds of this vast evergreen blanket that surrounded me, hoping God would meet me there, hoping for some gift of insight.

But it seemed the only gift from the forest that day was the peace I had received from the time I spent in its presence. That was something, a gift in its own way, and a gift I was thankful to receive. Getting up, I picked up a small pine cone, one from a Douglas fir, I later found out. It was not hard and brittle like most pine cones but supple instead, and its scales were overlapping each other and drawn in, as if to keep out the cold. I took it with me, dropping it off in my office and placing it on a bookshelf before I went home.

For the sake of the computer in my office, I kept the heat on all night. When I returned the next morning, it was cozy and warm. As I passed the bookshelf on the way to my desk, I glanced at the pine cone. Overnight it had changed. The scales had all spread out and opened up. I wondered. Was this the gift from the forest that I had prayed to find there yesterday? The pine cone had been closed when it was out in the cold, but it opened up in the warmth of my office.

It opened up in the warmth.

Opening up to warmth is the way the natural order works. It works that way because the word of God ordained it to work that way. Had He ordained the spiritual order to work that way, too? It seemed to me, as I reflected on it, that He had.

I decided to respond with warmth and forgiveness.

And not overnight but gradually, the pine cone started to open.

I returned to the reservoir another day, and on the way down I got a different view than I got going up. I noticed how beautiful the diagonals of rock were that jutted skyward. I wondered how it happened and how many years ago it happened. I imagined how violently it must have been thrust through the earth, rock shearing rock, splintering, colliding as the earth pitched and rolled. Great hulks of gray breaching the surface like a pod of whales, crashing down with enormous force. What deafening noise must have rent the silence here once a long time ago. What devastation was wrought, and yet, by the weathering grace of God, what beauty remains.

The juxtaposition of those two images—devastation and beauty—brought Psalm 46 to my mind.

God is our refuge and strength,
an ever-present help in trouble.
Therefore we will not fear, though the earth give way
and the mountains fall into the heart of the sea,
though its waters roar and foam
and the mountains quake with their surging.

There is a river whose streams make glad the city of God,
the holy place where the Most High dwells.
God is within her, she will not fall;
God will help her at break of day.
Nations are in uproar, kingdoms fall;
he lifts his voice, the earth melts.

The LORD Almighty is with us;
the God of Jacob is our fortress.

Come and see the works of the LORD,
the desolations he has brought on the earth.
He makes wars cease to the ends of the earth;
he breaks the bow and shatters the spear,
he burns the shields with fire.
"Be still, and know that I am God;
I will be exalted among the nations,
I will be exalted in the earth."

The LORD Almighty is with us;
the God of Jacob is our fortress.

That psalm in the Scriptures and that psalm from the side of the mountain on the way down from the reservoir, came together for me in such a way as to frame a window of the past year. Through that window I could see the devastation. The upheaval forever altered the landscape of my soul. But squinting, I could also see something of the beauty that was beginning to emerge.

In *A River Runs Through It*, Norman Maclean's father, a Presbyterian minister, is sitting on the banks of the river, reading the gospel of John while his sons are fishing. When Norman comes over to where he is sitting, the father pensively remarks: "In the part I was reading it says the Word was in the beginning, and that's right. I used to think water was first, but if you listen carefully you will hear that the words are underneath the water."

Underneath the Creation are the words of life, "Let there be. . . . and there was." Underneath the Exodus are words of deliverance. Underneath the wilderness, words of judgment. It was the word of God that brought forth manna. By a word of God, Israel was led out of the wilderness, and by another word, Moses was left behind.

God's words are underneath everything. And if you listen carefully, you will hear them.

I was fishing in Cheeseman Canyon where aeons ago a mountain parted to make room for this regal procession of water. It is one of the most beautiful places I know, and there are few places I would rather be, especially in the fall. I was standing knee-deep in the stream as the water curled around my waders. I worked the line on my rod, lifting the fly off the water and feathering it back. The river's voice was quiet, its lilting inflections rising to a gurgle, then falling to a murmur, rising, falling, speaking, calling.

What words were underneath these waters? *What was the river saying? And what, if anything, was it saying to me?*

"Eventually, all things merge into one, and a river runs through it," wrote Maclean as he was concluding his book. What the psalmist writes is a little different. Eventually, all things merge into oblivion. All things on earth, that is. But in heaven stands the city of God, and a river runs through it. One of the things the river offers the city is its gladness.

As I stood listening to the river that runs through Cheeseman Canyon, I could hear something of that gladness, or thought I could.

The world we live in, from the small worlds that are my life and yours to the great wide world we all live in, will one day come crumbling in around us. In the midst of that upheaval, the psalmist says: "Be still, and know that I am God."

It is not my nature to be still. By nature, I am a nail-biter who talks to himself all day long with a babble of Post-It Notes and a scribble of To-Do Lists. The river helped me to be still. And in helping me to be still, it helped me to realize who God is. So did Psalm 46. The Lord Almighty, He is the one who is with us. The God of Jacob, He is the one who is our fortress. He sees all that shakes . . . and remains unshaken. He sits above all that changes . . . and remains unchanged. In my anxiety I had forgotten that. The river helped me remember.

He sits enthroned in the city of God, and a river runs through it.

The river offers different things to different people.

To the boy on its banks, it offered sunfish.

To the man, it offered stillness.

And as I listen to the words underneath the waters, I think I hear something else. I think I hear the first spluttering syllables . . .

. . . of gladness.

A Prayer for Learning

Help me, O God,

To learn the beautiful language of Nature
so I too might be able to read
"the manuscripts of God."
Give me a hearing heart
so I might understand what I read,
And a humble heart
so I might learn even from the ants
how better to live my life . . .

Conclusion

A story is told of a carefree young girl who lived at the edge of a forest, where she loved to play and explore and take long adventurous journeys. But one day she journeyed too deep into the forest and got lost. As the shadows grew long, the girl grew worried. So did her parents. They searched the forest for her, cupping their hands and calling out. But there was no answer. In the gathering night the parents' search grew more intense.

The little girl tried one path after another, but none looked familiar and none led her home. Her skin was welted from the switching of limbs as she pushed her way through the overgrowth. Her knees were scraped from tripping in the dark. Her face was streaked from the tears she had cried. She called for her parents, but the forest seemed to swallow her words. After hours of trying to find her way home, the exhausted girl came to a clearing in the forest where she curled up on a big rock and fell asleep.

By this time the parents had enlisted the help of friends and neighbors, even strangers from town, to help them search for their lost little girl. In the course of the night many of the searchers went home. But not the girl's father. He searched all night and on into the next morning. In the first light of dawn he spotted his daughter asleep on the rock in the middle of the clearing. He ran as fast as his legs would take him, calling her name. The noise startled the girl awake. She rubbed her eyes. And reaching out to him, she caught his embrace.

"Daddy," she exclaimed, "I found you!"

The little girl awoke, rubbed her eyes, reached out her arms. "Daddy, I found you!"

That is what happens at windows of the soul. God searching for us and enlisting any help He can to find us. Running to us. Calling to us. And in a startling moment of awareness, we rub our eyes, reach out our arms, and find Him who for so long has been searching for us.

215

He searches for us on the Damascus road or the Emmaus road or whatever road we happen to be traveling at the time, even the pathless road through the forest where we have wandered and ended up lost. He meets us at a rock in the clearing or at a well outside a city in Samaria. He reaches out to us when we're out on a limb in some sycamore tree, the way he did with Zacchaeus, and receives us in the dark, the way he did Nicodemus. He may meet us where we work, charting stars in the heavens or counting sheep in the fields or writing study guides in the office. He may meet us in a dream as we sleep or in the Scriptures as we have our morning devotions.

There is no forest so deep that He cannot find us, no night so dark that He cannot see us in all our fears, all our tears, curled up in all our exhaustion.

Windows of the soul is where God finds us, or where we find Him, depending on whose point of view we're looking from, the father's or the little girl's. He comes to us where we are, speaks to us in our own language, calls us by our name.

It could be argued, though, that to open the possibility of God's speaking through other means than the clear teaching of Scripture is to let in all sorts of confusion. After all, a window lets in pollen along with the breeze, flies along with the sunshine, the cackle of crows along with the cooing of doves.

If that were your argument, I would have to agree.

But if we want fresh air, we have to be willing to live with a few flies.

Of course, we can shut out the flies and the pollen and the cackle of crows. And if a clean and quiet house is what's most important to us, perhaps that is what we should do. But if we do, we also shut out so much of the warmth, so much of the fragrance, so many of the sweet songs that may be calling us.

The flies are all obvious, but what besides the flies is coming to us through those windows?

What is God saying to us there? To you and to me?

Where is He calling us? To what vocation? To what wilderness or out of what wilderness?

What story is He wanting to tell with the reluctant heroes that are you and I?

What art is He wanting to create from the empty canvas of our lives?

What sculpture is He trying to craft from the rough-cut stone of who we are?

What poem is He wanting to write out of the painful images from our past?

What is He saying to you and to me through the images that flash across the screen of a theater or the images that flash across the screen of our soul as we sleep?

What dream is God dreaming when He dreams about you and about me, and how can we help that dream come true?

What memories is He bringing down from the attic? And why them, why now?

What is He showing us about ourselves through the pages of our diaries or through the pages of Scripture?

What people is He using in our lives, and what is He trying to tell us through them?

What word is He wanting to incarnate in our lives?

Where is He taking us with our tears, and do we have the courage to follow?

What wound is He healing in us through nature or what far-off horizon is He showing us through the music we hear?

What natural beauty is He wanting to bring out in you and in me?

What song is He wanting to sing with all the high and low notes of our lives?

In the past, God's word has come through tablets of stone and handwriting on a wall and through the pages of Scripture. It has come through a flood and a rainbow, a burning bush and a whirling wind. Through the correction of the prophets and the curses of Shemei. His word has thundered from Sinai and whimpered from a manger. His word has come through a dream in the night and a vision in the day. Through the mouths of kings and the mouths of babes. Through the psalms of God's anointed and the poems of pagans. Through a star in the night and through angels in the field. Through the birds of the air and the flowers of the field. Through a poor widow's offering, the picture of a good Samaritan, and the story of a prodigal son. His word was spoken through the law of Moses and afterward, more eloquently, through the life of Christ.

We live by those words, and on those words, not by bread alone but by every word that proceeds from the mouth of God. Some of those words are spoken at the most unexpected of places that if we're not expecting, we'll miss. Some of those words are spoken by the unlikeliest of people whom we will most likely dismiss if we don't receive them. And some of those words come in the most uncommon of ways that we will react against if we're not accustomed to the unaccustomed ways that God speaks.

Those words are the daily bread of our soul.

We have the responsibility to handle them accurately. But we have a more important responsibility. To handle them reverently. For they are words from the King. However they come, through whatever messenger they come, they are *His* words, and we should receive them as such.

I saw a reflection of this truth glinting off a small pool of Tennyson's words. The scene is King Arthur's castle, where he is knighting a handful of loyal men who would be called upon to risk their lives in his service.

> *Arthur sat*
> *Crown'd on the dais, and his warriors cried,*
> *"Be thou the king, and we will work thy will*
> *Who love thee." Then the King in low deep tones,*
> *And simple words of great authority,*
> *Bound them by so strait vows to his own self,*
> *That when they rose, knighted from kneeling, some*
> *Were pale as at the passing of a ghost,*
> *Some flush'd, and others dazed, as one who wakes*
> *Half-blinded at the coming of a light.*
>
> *But when he spake and cheer'd his Table Round*
> *With large, divine, and comfortable words,*
> *Beyond my tongue to tell thee—I beheld*

From eye to eye thro' all their Order flash
A momentary likeness of the King....

What we hear at windows of the soul may daze us or delight us. It may cause us to fall to our knees in fear or jump to our feet in joy. Sometimes what we hear at those windows is merely something to help us understand people more deeply or experience life more fully. Other times, what we hear are simple words of great authority that God has spoken.

It seems only appropriate to kneel in the presence of such words.

It seems too that these words, which are often beyond the human tongue to tell, should produce in us something beyond the rousing of our curiosity or the wakening of our wonder. It seems they should produce in us what they produced in Arthur's knights—a momentary likeness of the King—so that you and I and all of us gathered around the table of our Lord might be able to cry out with one voice:

"Be thou the king, and we will work thy will
Who love thee . . ."